JB
C6753
R9

SEP   2006

0429 411428

NAT KING COLE

Marianne Ruuth

MELROSE SQUARE PUBLISHING COMPANY
LOS ANGELES, CALIFORNIA

MARIANNE RUUTH lives in Los Angeles from where she reports, with emphasis on the cinema, for newspapers and magazines in France, Portugal, Scandinavia and other European countries. She is a former president of the Hollywood Foreign Press Association and the author of numerous books, fiction as well as non-fiction, including *Stevie Wonder; Eddie (Eddie Murphy from A to Z); Triumph and Tragedy, The True Story of the Supremes;* and *Cruel City, The Dark Side of Hollywood's Rich and Famous.* A contributing writer and researcher for *The Chronicle of the Twentieth Century* and *The Chronicle of America,* she has chaired Women in Film International and is a member of Mensa.

Consulting Editor for Melrose Square
Raymond Friday Locke

Originally published by Holloway House, Los Angeles.

Cover Painting: Harry Ahn
Cover Design: Jefferson Hitchcock
Original Pen/Ink Drawings: Christopher De Gasperi

NAT KING
COLE

MELROSE SQUARE BLACK AMERICAN SERIES

ELLA FITZGERALD
singer
NAT TURNER
slave revolt leader
PAUL ROBESON
singer and actor
JACKIE ROBINSON
baseball great
LOUIS ARMSTRONG
musician
SCOTT JOPLIN
composer
MATTHEW HENSON
explorer
MALCOLM X
militant black leader
CHESTER HIMES
author
SOJOURNER TRUTH
antislavery activist
BILLIE HOLIDAY
singer
RICHARD WRIGHT
writer
ALTHEA GIBSON
tennis champion
JAMES BALDWIN
author
JESSE OWENS
olympics star
MARCUS GARVEY
black nationalist leader
SIDNEY POITIER
actor
WILMA RUDOLPH
track star
MUHAMMAD ALI
boxing champion
FREDERICK DOUGLASS
patriot & activist
MARTIN LUTHER KING, JR.
civil rights leader

CONTENTS

I'm
Hurtin'

(song recorded by Nat King Cole in 1951)

The spotlight illuminated the elegant, tall man with the perfect posture as he took center stage. "Every inch a king," to quote Shakespeare. Nat King Cole's huge smile sparkled, his wide-set slanted eyes shone, as he, having been introduced as the star attraction, went into an inspired rendition of his first number, "Autumn Leaves," spicing it with an extra lilt. The audience broke into thunderous applause as the song ended.

The show was part of a series of one-nighters all through the South. In the tour were also the popular British band leader Ted Heath

---

Nat King Cole's music and stage persona made audiences love him. His inbuilt sense of true dignity would have made him the King, even if his name had been Smith rather than Cole...

with his 18-piece orchestra, his singer June Christy, Nat King Cole's trio (John Collins, Charlie Harris and Lee Young) and comedian Gary Morton.

They had been in Texas and played to audiences where the whites were sitting on one side and the blacks on the other side of the auditorium. The preceding evening they had delighted a segregated audience of seven thousand at a charity performance in Mobile.

Coming to perform in Alabama meant something special to Nat King Cole who was born in the state. Standing on the stage of the Municipal Auditorium in Birmingham the night of April 10, 1956, a tingling, almost intoxicating, joyous triumph was welling up inside him, as more than 3,500 faces were turned expectantly up toward him.

All of the faces were white. The state was segregated, but that was no news to him. He and his trio had performed there before, with the Big Show of 1951, traveling in a red, white and blue bus which patriotic colors did not transcend the black and white color lines. There had been some rumblings back then, especially since he had included a white bongo player, Jack Constanzo, in his group. (In some places it was okay for performers to be of different races but the audience could not mix;

in others even seeing different hues of skin color on a stage was upsetting.) Segregation and racism kept smarting, but he believed them to be symptoms of ignorance and misunderstandings rather than of actual evil. He also believed that music and the arts could be strong, magical bridges between people of all colors, nationalities, religions...

While looking forward to the late show for his black brothers and sisters, knowing that the atmosphere would be permeated by a special home feeling then, he enjoyed giving whole-heartedly and generously of his special gift to the white folks. He had been given the ability to inspire, relax and create positive dreams and aspirations in audiences, white and black, and he was going to use his gift to the fullest.

His second number was "Little Girl," which he delivered in his musky-voiced baritone, feeling strong rapport with the audience although he could not see them well beyond the bright flood of the spotlights.

He had just started the second chorus when a wolf howl erupted from the back of the auditorium. He kept singing, increasing both volume and intensity, as there seemed to be some commotion back there. Vaguely he distinguished sounds of feet thumping the

Racism reared its ugly head repeatedly during Cole's life, sometimes but not always draped in the white robes of the Ku Klux Klan. He chose to fight it through his art, seeing

racism as a symptom of ignorance rather than of evil, even after an ugly incident in Alabama, when members of White Citizens Councils attempted to carry him off a concert stage.

wooden floor of the auditorium. Suddenly something hit him. Momentarily blinded by the strong light, all he could see was a couple of eyes like black holes in a pale face, a grinning mouth. A generations-old, inbred fear enveloped him, followed by sharp pain.

The astonished audience had seen four men rush forward, crossing the ten feet between front row and stage, plunging over the footlights, mounting the high stage, one of them swinging on Cole and sending him reeling onto the piano bench with such force that it split under him.

The police in Birmingham had been tipped off that a demonstration of some sort was coming, but they had thought any potential demonstrators would use the steps at the end of the stage. Temporarily caught off base, about eight or ten policemen rushed in from the wings. One attacker, who had grabbed Cole's foot and was twisting it with all his might, was wrestled down to the floor while another swung at one of the cops and got a night stick across his head in return.

The minute the tumult started, the British orchestra had started up with a valiant rendition of "My Country 'tis of Thee" (luckily the tune is the same as "God Save the Queen").

The policemen escorted the handcuffed four

out of the auditorium. They were Willie Richard Vinson, 23, E.L. Vinson, 25, Kenneth Adams, 35, and Jesse W. Mabry, 43. Nat was brought backstage, the curtain rustled shut, and comedian Gary Morton went out to tell the audience that Nat King Cole could not continue the show. Someone in the audience shouted, "Please. . .please, ask him to come back so we can apologize." Shocked and still shaky, Cole limped back onto the stage and received a lengthy ovation. "At least five minutes," according to one eye witness.

He stood there, looking out at the sea of faces, reading shame and anger but also warmth and appreciation in them. "I just came here to entertain you. That was what I thought you wanted," he said simply in his soft voice with the perfect diction.

"We do! We do! Sing! Sing!" shouted members of the audience.

"Those folks hurt my back. I can't continue because I have to go to a doctor," he answered and walked off. Turning to a band member, he said with a sigh, "Man, I love show business, but I don't want to die for it."

He did remain in the theater in order to appear on stage again for the second show a couple of hours later. Grateful and proud, the blacks of the area responded to him with

Nat King Cole and his trio (Irving Ashby on guitar, Jack Constanzo on bongo drum, and Joe Comfort on bass) let loose

with rhythms that crept into the soul of the listeners. They appeared in musical vignettes in several films.

unbridled enthusiasm. "Sing it, Nat! Sing!"

Outside the auditorium, the police had found and arrested two men in a car (Orliss Clevenger, 18, and Mike Fox, 37) along with two .22 rifles, a blackjack, and a pair of brass knuckles.

The events leading up to the eruption of violence included a campaign by some White Citizens Councils against "decadent Negro music." They had been urging white patrons to boycott all such music. Investigation by Birmingham police brought evidence that the specific attack on Nat King Cole had been planned four days earlier in a filling station in Anniston, 60 miles from Birmingham. According to the plan, a mob of about 150 men, led by an officer of the North Alabama Citizens' Council (a die-hard segregationist group), was to have stormed the auditorium and carried Cole off. On the actual night, however, only these six showed up.

The mayor of Birmingham apologized publicly to the singer. The local newspaper, *Post-Herald,* called the attack "a warning to all of us that dangerously irresponsible forces are here, which, if given quarter, can result in nothing good for the community. . . If we are to have an orderly society, we must first have respect for the law. Those who trample it underfoot must be made to feel its certain penalty."

The penalty turned out to be rather mild for the six brutes: short jail sentences and minor fines. The presiding judge, Ralph E. Parker, commented in court that Cole had "observed our customs, traditions and laws, and his conduct was such as to win him many friends in the South."

Nat, although angry and frightened, had the rare wisdom and ability to look objectively at the incident, realizing that the attackers did not represent a majority. He told reporters afterwards that the audience was "wonderful" and "showed clearly they did not condone the action." He did add that he felt "befuddled" and "amazed," never having experienced anything like it ever before.

After the late show that night, he took off for Chicago to spend time with his father, refresh himself spiritually, and see a doctor about his foot and various bruises. There were no lasting injuries, and he rejoined the tour in Virginia a few days after the attack.

On April 18, he went on stage in Louisville, Kentucky, to sing to an audience of both blacks and whites. Ten thousand people rushed to their feet, clapping wildly, the moment he appeared.

Some blacks were criticizing him, saying he should not have joined up with the same tour again nor ever performed for segregated audiences. He told them, "I'm an entertainer, not a politician." He felt strongly that he could serve the case of blacks best by what he did and by continuing to perform for white audiences. It was his firm belief that the more the latter could feel inspired and entertained by a black person, the quicker deeply rooted attitudes would erode. He knew he couldn't come to the South for a few evenings and turn over the law, which was still the law of segregation. (It was exactly two weeks after the attack on him that the Supreme Court ruled that bus companies in the South could no longer force blacks to sit at the back of the bus.)

As the criticism continued, he stated that he would refuse to appear before segregated audiences in the future "if all other Negro musicians will join a boycott." That never happened.

Being a popular artist, meaning that every part of his life was open to scrutiny, he heard other negative voices, some focusing in on the fact that he had never joined the NAACP (the National Association for the Advancement of Colored People). The critics had failed to notice that, although not a formal member, he

In an early publicity photo manager Carlos Gastel sent out, the elegance, exuberance and sparkle of the "King" (at this time rather "the Prince of the Ivories") is evident.

had performed several times at NAACP benefits and contributed to various causes. Nat was hurt by the disapproval coming from his own people, including some harsh statements by Thurgood Marshall, at the time an outspoken civil rights lawyer and later appointed by President Johnson to the United States Supreme Court.

Nat did join the NAACP subsequently and was one of the strong supporters of the Reverend Martin Luther King, Jr.'s Southern Christian Leadership Conference.

Something good came out of the shameful evening:

Journalists began writing about the treatment of black artists.

Frank Sinatra spoke passionately against the attack and its underlying causes.

Some theological students in Florida used the violence directed against Nat King Cole as an example of what they must fight in the minds and hearts of their fellow human beings.

A number of musicians, with Nat visibly in front, petitioned the AFL-CIO to integrate the segregated musicians' locals of the American Federation of Musicians.

In Hollywood the talk of more opportunities for black actors in films increased.

June Christy was the singer with Ted Heath's orchestra during the 1956 tour throughout the South, when the vicious attack on Cole took place in Birmingham, Alabama.

Chapter Two

I'm A
Shy Guy

*(recorded by Nat King Cole, with Capitol
International Jazzmen, in 1945)*

"**I**t's a boy!"

It was St. Patrick's Day in Montgomery,
Alabama, "the cradle of Confederacy," the
First World War was just over, and the Jazz
Age was standing on the threshold, when the
Reverend Edward James Coles and his wife
Perlina, an accomplished pianist, greeted their
fourth child, Nathaniel Adams Coles, on
March 17, 1919.

The family, which included his sister Eddie
Mae, seven, his brother Edward James, six,
and little Evelyn, four, joined hands giving
prayers of thanksgiving that this newborn boy

---

*Nat's six year older brother Eddie was his inspiration and
influence from babyhood on. Eddie, who played many
instruments, encouraged Nat to learn to read music.*

looked healthy and strong. Perlina had given birth to several children who had not survived early infancy. She had experienced deep sorrow each time but had bowed her head in acceptance of what life dealt her.

Looking at her children, she would incessantly dream of a better life for them than what Alabama could offer, especially to blacks.

Edward Coles, a devoted but strict husband and father, was the minister of the Beulah Baptist Church. She herself was the daughter of a Baptist minister, the Reverend Dan Adams, and knew what was expected of a minister's wife. She led the gospel choir, and she raised her children as best she could, slowly and steadily influencing her husband to look for a better life up North. The small woman with expressive eyes and a quiet strength, coupled with a lot of compassion, succeeded in her wish in 1923, when baby Nat was four years old, and the family made the move to Chicago. There Edward Coles was to head his own church, the Second Progressive Baptist Church.

They took the train, traveling for two days and a night, nourished by the food Nat's mother had brought along but even more by their hope for more than the meager, segregated existence in Alabama. Chicago in the 1920s acted as a sort of magnet, attracting Southern blacks who sought a realistic chance to improve their lives.

The Coles family was living on the ground floor of an apartment building at Forty-First Street and Prairie Avenue on Chicago's South Side. Dominating their living room was a small upright piano on which Perlina gave her children music lessons. Young Nat was an eager pupil, always sporting bruises from falling off the piano bench but climbing right up again. The first song he played with two hands was "Yes, We Have No Bananas."

His brother Eddie, six years his senior, with whom he shared a room, was his idol. Eddie was a much more outgoing, assertive child than Nat, who was shy and spoke softly. Eddie was in constant trouble with their father about his taste in music since he preferred to leave the church music behind and try his hand at boogie-woogie or the popular songs of the day. Reverend Coles was ever warning that the devil was cleverly hiding many sinful temptations in the worldly music, but Eddie kept playing what he liked and listening to swinging music on the radio whenever his father was not around. Nat followed suit, quietly but stubbornly. Perlina was more liberal in these matters, being a firm believer in the importance

In Birmingham, Alabama, Nat and his group were assaulted by a gang of white racists as they were performing in front of an all white audience. During the second chorus of "Little Girl,"

four men rushed the stage and swung at Cole, knocking him into his piano. The members of the audience apologized afterwards for the conduct of those men, encouraging Nat to go on.

of a child playing an instrument with joy and having a love and understanding of music. "Music is the heart of culture," she told her children, consistently encouraging the musical bent evident in them.

Nat's father was taking his role as parent seriously, preaching to his children about the righteous way to live. Each meal began with saying grace and ended with thanksgiving. It was a strict upbringing where the reverend's leather belt left stinging marks on various buttocks, but theirs was also a close-knit family where talking and joking were part of everyday life.

Nothing could hold Eddie back. Barely in his teens, he began to work professionally. He would wait until the family was asleep and then jump out a window and go to his engagements, where he played piano, bass, and tuba. Nat was watching, keeping his mouth loyally shut about it, and learning.

He had to learn a devastating lesson at about age ten, when his seventeen-year-old sister Eddie Mae took sick during the harsh winter, developed pneumonia and died. Evelyn, who was fourteen, comforted Nat; she was doting on him like a miniature mother. His father told them that the tragedy was God's will which had to be accepted, and life went on.

Coles was a good preacher who attracted churchgoers so he moved his church to larger rooms at Forty-Fifth Street and Deerborn and changed its name to the True Light Baptist Church.

At about this time Nat entered a musical contest at a local theater and won first prize, a Thanksgiving turkey, which he brought home to his proud mother.

Nat, the diplomat in the family, played the church organ for his father's service, alternating with singing in the choir, but in his free time he was drawn toward the world of jazz, and he was beginning to follow Eddie out of their bedroom window, going to clubs and listening to the fine musicians the city had to offer. The clubs and the radio made him familiar with a galaxy of great artists, and, most of all, with the pianist Earl "Fatha" Hines, who was leading his own band at a Chicago club and whose performances were often broadcast on the radio.

Nat Cole said later that listening to the forever inventing and embellishing Hines opened a lot of doors in his mind and gave him countless ideas about music. He was influenced to the extent that he went into jazzy improvisations in the middle of playing the gospel music during his father's services and was repeatedly told to "tone it down."

His mother, sensing her son's tremendous talent, worked out a compromise. If Nat would continue to play and sing in church, he should be able to try for work as a jazz pianist on week nights, she told her husband who agreed, albeit reluctantly.

As Eddie and Nat were getting into the professional music world, Evelyn was also playing the organ well, and she loved to dance, which her father forbade her to do. She obeyed him, most of the time.

Eddie, concentrating on the bass at this time, was proud of his little brother and a good influence. He told Nat to learn to read music because without that skill he would never get jobs with the big bands. At first reluctant to deal with scales and chords, Nat took his brother's word for the necessity to learn the technical side in order to become more versatile. From age twelve he did study the classics, playing everything from Bach to Rachmaninoff.

At Wendell Phillips High School in the heart of the South Side black community, a youth band was organized, and Nat was so determined to get into it that he learned any instrument at all (possibly tuned bells) to be accepted, the youngest of all.

Music and baseball were Nat's big loves in high school. He liked football too but not as much as baseball. He became a first baseman and was even toying with the idea of becoming a professional. A couple of minor-league clubs were interested, as his father proudly recalled in 1960 when, on January 6, Nat was featured on the television program *This Is Your Life.* Although music and show business won out, he remained a lover of sports all his days.

He became friends with the guitarist Les Paul, then nineteen (four years older than Nat), and the two went to every club in the area. Les, who was white, had to go to the South Side in order to meet and play with the black musicians he admired, including Earl Hines and Louis Armstrong, because they hardly ever ventured into white neighborhoods.

At age sixteen, Nat organized not one but two musical groups—a big band (over ten pieces), Nat Coles and His Rogues of Rhythm, and a quintet, Nat Coles and His Royal Dukes. He played in and led whichever group he could find a job for.

Music was his passion, he was a musician— the only singing he did was in church, and he didn't particularly like doing it. He agreed with his contemporaries who kidded him about his "horrible" voice. He was still shy, to the point that he often asked his sister Evelyn to come along to gigs. He had shot up to six feet and girls liked him, but he became tongue-tied around them. Evelyn, whom he called "Bay," was there as a buffer and a shield.

From an early age, an uninhibited passion for music reigned in his soul coupled with a remarkable affinity with the piano. He admired Duke Ellington, Art Tatum, Fats Waller, and, most of all and always, Earl "Fatha" Hines.

In an interview with John Tynan (*Down Beat* magazine in 1957), he said, "It was his driving force that appealed to me. I first heard Hines in Chicago when I was a kid. He was regarded as the Louis Armstrong of piano players. His was a new, revolutionary kind of playing, because he broke away from the Eastern style. He broke the barrier of what we called stride piano where the left hand kept up in a steady, striding pattern. I latched onto that new Hines style. Guess I still show that influence to this day."

He also liked Jimmie Noone's band, especially Noone's theme song, "Sweet Lorraine," which song would be one of his own big hits later on.

Maria and Nat Cole adopted her niece Carol when the little girl's mother died. Carol, called "Cookie," turned to acting as a young adult and appeared in The Owl and the Pussycat.

The brothers Nat and Eddie talked music, played music, analyzed music, let themselves be brought to mental and spiritual highs by music. Eddie was an outgoing person who got to know a lot of the jazz musicians personally and thus met Noble Sissle, the band leader who, along with the pianist Eubie Blake, had created hits on Broadway. Sissle offered Eddie a job in his Society Orchestra. Over his father's strong protests, Eddie went on the road, traveling around the country and even to Europe. While he was away, Nat dove into classical, jazz, gospel—it all worked together and made him develop his own distinct style.

He urged his groups to take just about any job offered, whatever the pay, for the purpose of learning and becoming a little more known each time they appeared.

He remained shy but was also disarmingly friendly, with a unique ability to listen to and understand others. People liked him. "A really sweet guy," was the general opinion.

Big bands used to have contests at the Savoy ballroom on Sundays. Nat's big band went up against Earl Hines' band and, despite all the fine musicians in Hines' band, the high school guys won. This led to Nat's group being hired for dances at the Savoy, and to Nat being at times referred to as "the Prince of the Ivories"

(Hines remained the King).

The following year, Eddie returned from having toured Europe, coming back with an international flair and the ability to speak foreign languages. He had decided that he wanted to stay in Chicago and get a music degree from the university.

The Coles moved into a house at 1412 Greenfield in North Chicago as Reverend Coles became head of the First Baptist Church. Two new babies had been welcomed into the family: Isaac, called Ike, was born in 1927, and Lionel, whom everyone called Freddy, in 1931. Both boys were showing signs of following in their brothers' footsteps, already loving jazz and blues. The poor reverend might have been baffled as he watched every son of his grow up to become a professional musician, especially since there were preachers and deacons on both sides of the family. Why didn't anyone of them want to become a preacher? he wondered. But he did appreciate that they all got along famously, always encouraging each other, praising each other's qualities. They were all talented, and there seemed to be hardly any jealousy or competition between them.

Playing music at night, jamming at clubs into the wee hours, and going to school at day just became too much for Nat. So he quit high school without getting his diploma in order to devote all his time to music. He was clearly a unique talent; even his parents realized that and made no fuss about him quitting school. It certainly was not laziness that forced his decision because he was working and studying harder than ever.

Eddie was impressed by how far Nat had progressed, and the two merged some of the musicians in Nat's groups into a sextet, Eddie Cole's the Solid Swingers, with Nat at the piano (both brothers dropped the final "s" from their name at this time, although they never bothered to make the change legally). They managed to get a six-month engagement at the Panama Club on Fifty-eighth Street, and Nat earned eighteen dollars a week. Eddie also got the group a recording date with Decca's Sepia Series which made records especially for blacks. They recorded four sides (in July of 1936): "Honey Hush"/"Thunder" and "Bedtime"/"Stomping at the Panama." It didn't make them rich but it boosted their standing in the community—and their egos.

The year was 1945 and Duke Ellington was broadcast inter-
nationally over Voice of America. Nat idolized Ellington, and
Maria Cole had been one of Ellington's vocalists.

Chapter Three

If I Give My Heart To You

(recorded by Nat King Cole in 1954)

The brothers and their Solid Swingers went on a tour to the South but were stranded along the way and had to put their instruments as collateral to get their bus driver to take them back to Chicago.

There a revival production of *Shuffle Along*, a show that Noble Sissle and Eubie Blake had brought to success already in the 1920s (the first all black show to make it to Broadway), was going into rehearsal. Both Eddie and Nat found work in the show. So did one Nadine Robinson, a petite chorus-line dancer in her late twenties originally from St. Louis, whom

---

Dizzy Gillespie was another young musician put under contract by Capitol Records in the formative days of the company. He went on to become one of the great jazz musicians of his era.

Nat had first met at the Panama Club. Nat was attracted both to her beauty (she was striking looking with light brown eyes contrasting with her dark skin, which, however, was not as dark as Nat's), and her maturity (she was about ten years older than he) which meant that she had more show business experience than he had.

After playing six weeks in Chicago, *Shuffle Along* was going on the road. Eddie quit the show, but Nadine wanted to go on. And then Nat wanted to go, too. The two brothers had many heated arguments because Eddie wanted to keep Nat in Chicago with the Solid Swingers. This turned into the worst fight of their life, but the love-stricken Nat insisted on going, packed his bag and went.

The tour involved a lot of work and hardships, especially since many hotels did not accept blacks. As a result, the cast members were frequently sleeping in (unheated) theaters.

In spite of the discomfort, love bloomed between Nat and Nadine, and they decided to get married. They made all the proper arrangements but couldn't wait and got married impulsively in Ypsilanti, Michigan, by a judge. Two days later, they arrived at the home of the people who had made specific arrangements for their wedding—and went through the whole thing again.

Two months after leaving Chicago, the troupe arrived in Long Beach, California, where they were to perform at the New Strand Theater. Misfortune struck. Somebody stole the payroll of almost a thousand dollars, audiences stayed away, and everyone in the show was out of a job.

Across from the theater was a small restaurant where a group of musicians was playing nightly, and, having heard him tackle the piano, they invited Nat to come and play with them. This helped a little, but things were still hard for the two newlyweds with no funds. While the rest of the company returned to Chicago, Nat and Nadine stayed on. They loved the climate, the sunshine and the palm trees, and besides, he did not want his father to see him doing poorly nor, perhaps, face Eddie who had turned out to be right about the tour. Also, Nadine was confident that Nat would do better in California than in Chicago.

"I played practically every beer joint in Los Angeles and around, from San Diego to Bakersfield, never making more than $5 at night," he said later. "But it wasn't so bad, you know. At that age, nobody worries. Nothing is going to scare a kid sixteen or seventeen years old out of the idea he is going to be rich and famous.''

A relative of Nadine's had a house which they rented cheaply. So he kept playing where he could, on whatever instruments were available, often out-of-tune pianos with which he had to struggle, and went jamming in the downtown clubs afterwards. The local musicians liked the unassuming, dark young man with his contemporary, rhythmic style at the piano. ''That cat can play!'' was the word spreading around town, and he found jobs as rehearsal pianist and even occasionally as studio pianist for a guy named Frankovich, who later changed his name to Frankie Laine and became immensely popular.

Nadine took odd jobs dancing or being hostess in clubs in the area. The couple bought a used car. Later Nadine recalled this as a happy time despite the lack of money. . .a time of long walks, of discovering the city, of singing together and writing songs together.

In retrospect, success seems to have come easily to Nat Cole, but in reality things were tough for a long time. People who remember seeing him in 1938 recall an intense, music-obsessed Nat, looking even younger than his eighteen or nineteen years, undernourished, and with threadbare clothes, although they were always kept immaculately clean and pressed by Nadine so that he looked sharp in spite of it all.

About this time he sat down and wrote the whimsical song about the monkey who took a sky-ride on a buzzard, refusing to let go and fall to his death. The story came from a parable his father sometimes used in a sermon. The message of the story and the song was: Don't give up. Hold on to your principles and do your best. "Straighten up and fly right," he called it, which was what his father used to tell the congregation, and the words were a constant inspiration to Nat, who regarded his father with admiration and respect. Nat sold the song for fifty dollars, outright, no royalties. It was a matter of paying the rent.

In 1937 he had figured out the simple mathematics that three men available for jobs could get more work than one man—and perhaps even more than a larger band that might be too expensive for a small club.

It was probably in 1938 Nat put together his first trio—or at least that was the year they first played together professionally. Nat had gone to different clubs to find just the right musicians since the owner of old Sewanee Inn on North La Brea had promised to try them out. From Lionel Hampton's group, just disbanding, he recruited Wesley Prince, the bassist (also a minister's son, coming from a musical family, about twelve years older than Nat), and Oscar Moore, a guitarist with charisma (he played the guitar when Mickey Rooney pretended to do so in the film *Girl Crazy;* he also came from a musical family and was three or four years older than Nat). The three of them—and sometimes but not always with the addition of a drummer—played at Sewanee for a weekly salary of seventy-five dollars which they split three ways.

And how did he become the King?

There are several stories. One says that a drunk crowned him "king" with a paper hat. Another that Bob Lewis, the manager of the club, was so delighted with Nat's singing that he put a gold leaf crown on Nat's head, calling him King Cole, an easily understandable sobriquet from the nursery rhyme about Old King Cole. The trio began to call themselves the King Cole Swingsters, which name evolved to the King Cole Trio, and their popularity was growing. When they included a drummer, people used to call them Nat King Cole and His Swingsters Three.

But how did this musician become the *singing* King?

True or not, this is how the legend tells it.

As Nat and his colleagues played their instrumentals, a tipsy customer hollered, "Sing!" He went on pleading loudly with Nat to sing "Sweet Lorraine." Nat told him gently that the group was purely instrumental; no singers. The drunk insisted. The manager rushed up and said, "This guy's a big spender. So sing already!"

Nat shrugged and sang "Sweet Lorraine," feeling his way every inch, aware that his range was limited and he had to make up for the "furry" sound of his voice by meticulous phrasing and perfect timing.

The Sewanee regulars loved it. This was a new side of their favorite piano player. Some liked his singing specifically because they could hear every syllable and the tune was not interfered with.

Of course, Nat liked to tell another version of the story: An insistent customer wanted him to sing, and he finally gave in, whereupon the customer tipped the trio fifteen cents. After the song, Nat asked if the man wanted something else, and the man said, "Yeah, I'd like my three nickels back..."

After the Sewanee Inn, the trio worked at Jim Otto's Steak House and a few other places. "We were the first group of any kind to break into the cocktail lounges out there," Nat said

As success hit, Hollywood took notice of his popularity. The Nat King Cole Trio, with Nat at the piano, were seen and

heard in films such as *Pistol-Packing Mama* (released in 1943) starring Ruth Terry (shown) and Robert Livingston.

later. "Bob Lewis took a chance, gave us a chance, and the breaks were right and we did all right." In several of these clubs they were the first blacks ever to perform.

A lot of clubs were all-white, barring black people from attending, but in some cases it was all right if the performers were black. Whites could go to the black clubs, however, and more and more of them did, drawn by the magic of the music.

Nadine and Nat seemed to get along well; she managed to cook great soul food dinners for little money and always welcomed his friends. Nat began talking about having children, dreaming of becoming a father, but she seemed to be unable to carry a pregnancy to its end. She suffered a couple of miscarriages over the years.

He was always busy with his music (whatever else was happening, he practiced a minimum of two hours per day), and in between he was an easygoing man who didn't complain nor criticize nor argue with her.

He worked on routines in which the other two musicians joined in his singing or made humorous exclamations, sometimes he wrote playful lead-in dialogues; people loved them, and their combined salary went up to $110 a week.

After hours he was jamming with other people. This was a way for musicians to get to know each other, and the informal jam sessions often led to jobs. But the musicians' union, the black local 767 (the union was not as yet integrated), prohibited jamming as they didn't want artists to perform for free. Finally the ingenious musicians convinced the union to let them jam in a rehearsal hall just above the union offices. Every afternoon great music poured out of that room, but it was so loud that the building vibrated and nobody could work. They were asked to leave—and had no more problems about jamming at clubs late at night.

There were always women around. Groupies tend to hang around good musicians, even poverty-stricken ones. This caused a bit of a problem for Oscar Moore (it actually broke up his marriage), but even though Nat Cole had some problems with overly insistent female admirers, he seemed to be able to handle it.

In 1938 the trio recorded a song, "There's No Anesthetic for Love," exactly as they performed it in the club with Nat as the doctor. The song conveyed the feeling of fun that permeated the trio's work. Each recording added to the popularity they were experiencing to an increasing degree.

By 1940, Nat was thinking of joining up with

the Lionel Hampton band, and he did record with Hampton for Decca—seven tunes with him on piano and Oscar Moore on guitar. It went well, and Cole's Swingsters went back in the summer to record four more songs, including "Sweet Lorraine," "Gone With the Draft," "Honeysuckle Rose," and "This Side Up."

Cole's singing was attracting increased attention. His voice was masculine, easy to identify, a little hoarse, generally considered sexy. His phrasing was nothing less than marvelous. But primarily he was seen, by himself and others, as a pianist and a superb one. Singers liked to hire him to practice, and he would coach them, teaching them about the phrasing of songs and about showing respect for the lyrics.

He was also doing arrangements for friends and was getting a reputation for being a wonderful arranger with an ability to supply "a kick" for chorus-line dancers.

When Nat King Cole was honored in 1962, on his twenty-fifth anniversary, Mahalia Jackson came to his tribute at the Ambassador hotel and sang a spirited rendition of "Joshua."

Chapter Four

Pitchin' Up A Boogie

(recorded in 1943)

As Nat King Cole was becoming known locally, a booking agent set up a tour for his trio. They went to Dayton, Ohio, playing the 2800 Club; they went to Philadelphia and Washington, D.C.; and they went to Chicago, relieving Bob Crosby's band at the Sherman Hotel, playing Capitol Lounge and clubs such as the Blue Note. Although Nat liked to say jokingly, "Nobody knew we were there except our families," he felt good about returning to the city of his childhood with his own group. Always he seemed concerned that his parents, especially his father, should be proud of him.

Fabulous jazz singer Ella Fitzgerald, a contemporary of Nat Cole's, shared with him the quality of a style that seemed effortless and a compelling need to perform, to communicate.

In Chicago, they recorded for Decca in March of 1941 with Nat singing "Babo," "Scotchin' with the Soda" and "Slow Down." They also did one instrumental, "Early Morning Blues."

This stay meant a reunion with his family. None of them, except Eddie who had visited Nat and Nadine in Los Angeles during a tour with his new group, Three Loose Nuts and a Bolt, had seen Nat for four years, and they had not met Nadine until now. They all took to her from the start, and she stayed on with the family when Nat continued to tour.

In New York, Nat's trio played at Nick's in Greenwich Village and then landed an extended engagement at Kelly's Stable in midtown, more specifically on what was known as "Swing Street"—West 52nd Street. Billie Holiday was the headliner at Kelly's Stable when Nat first went there to play, his trio being the relief group. At this time the members of the trio wore co-ordinated sports clothes—later on, when they could afford it, they would settle on matching outfits.

Again, people applauded Nat and his soft rhythms—and not the least his singing, which was becoming more frequent even though instrumentals were still dominating the performances. However, his songs weren't playing on radio and could not consequently be classified as hits. Also, there exists conflicting information about how much singing he did at this time, one story claiming that they didn't know at Kelly's that he sang until somebody called up and told them; another source stating that he filled in for Billie Holiday on a couple of occasions when she was not feeling well.

Whenever not working, Nat went jamming in various clubs, getting to know the New York scene which included Count Basie, the Dorseys, Artie Shaw, Benny Goodman, Frank Sinatra...His only time off from music seems to have been when he went to watch football and baseball games, often hanging out with the athletes afterwards.

By the end of 1941, the trio was back in Los Angeles, now and then taking an engagement in another place, another state. In the City of Angels, they played various clubs such as Fox Hills Lounge (across from Fox studios), the Club Circle in Beverly Hills, and ended up in the Radio Room on Vine Street (across from NBC Studios in those days). The magazine *Down Beat* ran its first column on Cole about this time. "He plays all styles well, slow blues, boogie, and jump tunes."

One of his admirers was Johnny Mercer, the

gifted songwriter, who was working at NBC. "You must hear this guy! He's incredibly fascinating!" he told his friends and brought them to hear Nat. When Mercer helped to start Capitol Records, he brought Nat Cole into the company as one of its first artists. One recording, in which Nat did not sing, was with tenor saxophonist Lester Young and has come to be considered a classic with an absolutely spectacular performance by Nat in pieces such as "Indiana," "Tea for Two," "Body and Soul," and "I Can't Get Started."

The first recording that attracted widespread attention was "That Ain't Right," in 1941. The following year the trio went back to Kelly's Stable, where Billie Holiday was again the featured singer. The Nat King Cole Trio was paid $165 a week by this time.

They played also at the 331 Club, another step up the ladder of fame. Judy Garland, Lena Horne and Cab Calloway went there and even sat in with the group, just for the pleasure of the fluid, often surprising music the trio offered. The place was small, intimate, always crowded, and frequented by a lot of movie stars.

Many, including musicians, were drafted at this time, but Nat was classified as 4-F. (The story is that he either had "nervous hyper-

Sammy Davis, Jr. said: "He was the gentlest man I ever knew."
They shared an exuberant sense of humor and liked to "hang
out" after performances in Las Vegas or Lake Tahoe.

tension" or it was a matter of flat feet.)

He and his group kept recording, hoping for a resounding hit in the only market open to them, the so called "race" market, meaning the black market. Music and records were as segregated in those days as the society around them. A handful of female singers had managed a crossover: Billie Holiday, Ethel Waters, Ella Fitzgerald...but they were the exceptions.

Slowly, steadfastly, Nat's career was building, although no one could have known how high it would go. Perhaps he himself knew deep inside because it seems he never wavered in his climb upwards, driving from club to club in his worn, dented old car, playing whenever he had a chance, giving it his all, making friends in his easy-going way.

The record store named Wallichs' Music City was located at the corner of Sunset and Vine in the heart of Hollywood. Glen Wallichs, the owner, truly loved music and musicians, and from time to time he invited his favorites to record in the store. One day he invited Nat to do so, along with Harry "Sweets" Edison, a drummer named "Juicy" Owens, and George "Red Callender." (On the same date a tenor saxophonist was working there with other musicians—his name was Gordon Dexter.)

Some time in 1943, the King Cole Trio acquired a brilliant manager, Carlos Gastel, a native of Honduras, a go-getter of first class, a man who worked hard and played hard, affectionately called "the happy walrus" by his friends. It is estimated that the trio was earning about $225 a week when they met up with Gastel, who said that he would take no money from them until their earnings were up "around $800 a week." To Nat Cole, this figure sounded preposterous. "How will you ever make money if you put such a high figure on it?" he said to Gastel, as he was trying to talk him into taking a percentage of any earnings, all to make him really work hard at getting them out to play. Gastel refused and within a couple of weeks booked them into the Orpheum Theatre in Los Angeles—for one thousand dollars a week! Soon Gastel managed hardly anyone except Nat King Cole—and it has been said that these two men never signed a contract. A handshake did just fine.

"I knew the direction I wanted to travel in and realized Carlos could help me. . . I can honestly say that much of the success I enjoy today I owe to Carlos," Nat told *Down Beat* magazine later on.

Gastel got the trio an exclusive seven year recording contract with Capitol Records with a five percent royalty (which was the maximum allowed by the recording industry then and until the 1960s). Capitol, which had been formed by the aforementioned Glen Wallichs of Music City, a Paramount producer named Buddy DeSylva, and the prolific lyricist Johnny Mercer, bought the rights to some of the recordings Nat had done earlier for other companies.

There was not a lot of pressure from the Capitol owners. They were true music lovers, who admired and trusted both Nat Cole's musicality and good taste in choosing songs. They produced instrumentals as well as records with Nat singing. Among the latter were "Gee Baby, Ain't I Good To You," "Sweet Lorraine," "Embraceable You," "It's Only a Paper Moon," and "I Can't See You for Lookin'." Nat also recorded his own "Straighten Up and Fly Right" which became a huge hit. He didn't realize until after that fact that he had sold all rights to the song shortly after he wrote it when in dire financial circumstances. This meant that all royalties for music and lyrics went to Mills Music which had bought the song. It was a bitter experience for him, and yet, the song brought the King Cole Trio its first solid national fame.

Barbara McNair played the female lead in Cole's Broadway show, I'm With You. *Although the show received only lukewarm reviews, Barbara and Nat got along well, continuing their working relationship in a new version of the play called* Wandering Man.

Chapter Five

A Weaver Of Dreams

(recorded in 1952)

Commercial success had hit, but Nat King Cole, although finding himself a pop star, was combining this with being a jazz musician, and the trio kept playing regularly in local jazz clubs. Jazz musicians did not experience the same publicity nor the monetary success of pop stars.

A film editor named Norman Granz was a terrific jazz lover who had a dream: to arrange a major jazz concert in Los Angeles, in the Philharmonic Auditorium at Pershing Square. The date was set for July 2, 1944. The concert was to be recorded, and Nat Cole was in-

Nat King Cole ventured into acting. One of his roles was that of a French foreign legionnaire in the film China Gate, co-starring Angie Dickinson, Gene Barry and Lee Van Cleef.

vited to participate, tickling the black and white ivories. Since he had an exclusive recording contract with Capitol, he was technically not allowed to do this, but he decided to use a pseudonym for the concert—and chose the name Shorty Nadine ("Shorty" being his nickname for petite Nadine). Oscar Moore was going to play guitar as usual but, due to him falling for some young lady and refusing to leave wherever he was shacking up with her, Nat called Les Paul and asked him to sit in. Without the benefit of rehearsal Les Paul showed up, calling himself Paul Leslie, because he was with the Armed Forces Radio Service and was not supposed to play as a civilian.

The concert was a smash hit, not the least for Shorty Nadine and Paul Leslie who pulled out all stops and played inspiredly, almost frenziedly, to the point that people in the audience literally stood up in their seats, screaming their enthusiastic approval. The resulting recording became a jazz classic.

So what did Capitol do? Did they sue Nat for breaking his exclusive contract with them? Not at all. They realized that he would occasionally make forays into other labels (as Nature Boy or Eddie Laguna or Sam Schmaltz or A Guy or whatever name for himself he could think of) but always only as an instrumentalist, never as a singer. These were two different worlds, and it speaks well for the sensitivity and understanding on the part of the bosses at Capitol that they recognized that this man named Nat *was* music, had to play, and should not be fettered.

The trio did some radio work, including a couple of appearances on Orson Welles' show, impressing everyone with the way they found melodic variations, executing them perfectly.

When Capitol released Nat's "Gee Baby, Ain't I Good to You?" the song rose to the ninth place on the charts and stayed there (*Newsweek,* August 12, 1946).

In music magazine polls Nat King Cole began by ending up near the top until he more and more frequently took first place.

Privately Nat liked to kid about his own singing, the hoarse, breathy sound which had become his trademark, still amazed that people actually liked it. He thought it might be his way of telling a story in a song, his perfect pitch, his way of setting a mood, rather than his actual voice, that attracted listeners.

Ballads had become popular during the war years. White singers like Frank Sinatra, Bing Crosby and Perry Como became famous for their renditions of ballads, and it began to happen that a couple of black male singers made

Growing up in a world without mirrors... That's how it was when Nat King Cole grew up and few blacks were seen on television or in films. He wanted to change all that. He was a

guest star on shows hosted by Frank Sinatra and Bing Crosby but wanted to see blacks as hosts of their own shows and having prominent parts in good dramas and comedies.

the crossover and that slowly their soulful singing became popular with white audiences. One of these was Billy Eckstine...the other was Nat King Cole. This didn't happen overnight, of course. In the beginning, it was not considered fitting for white women's ears to be caressed by the velvety voices of black men singing love songs!

Remarkably enough, with the growing success, Nat's ego did not swell. In an interview with *The Saturday Evening Post* he said about his piano playing that "there's a lot of notes lying around on that old piano. I just pick the ones I like." Another time he said that his voice was "nothing to be proud of. It's maybe two octaves in range. I guess it's the hoarse, breathy noise that some like."

All through his fantastic career he tended to depreciate his part in his success, calling it "just the breaks." He would confide to friends that he didn't understand exactly how it had come about and why.

One reason was that he was always choosing his songs with care. They had to express genuine feeling, and he sang them with sincerity. Each one had to have a special meaning to him.

In Capitol's publicity publication *The Capitol,* the following description of him was delivered: "Cole is conscientious to the extreme; he practices singing and piano regularly, striving to improve both. He's never late on the job, and his personal habits might well be the model for a troop of Boy Scouts. No one in the music business is better liked..."

Hollywood began to take notice, and the Cole trio appeared in musical vignettes (which were cut out for releases in the South) in films such as *Here Comes Elmer, Pistol-Packing Mama, Under Western Skies, Killer Diller* as well as in short films, featuring one or two songs and aimed at black audiences via video jukeboxes.

The singing was taking over more and more; Nat was sacrificing his piano playing to the point where some people were almost forgetting what a virtuoso he was, but it was the singing that made him rich and famous, not the piano playing. Women were screaming when he sang about love—and that meant dollars in his pocket.

Another quote from Nat about his singing illustrates further how he felt about it: "A doctor heard me one night and told me: 'Son, with that throat you ought to be home in bed.' I'm a pretty good piano player, but I can't sing."

Critics agreed with his self-appraisal as a pianist. Some, in fact, took the position that it was a dirty trick of fate that made Nat so fabulous a singer that his piano work was sidetracked.

Going on tour, the trio broke attendance records in many places—and it was largely due to Nat's singing.

The publicity was increasing. *The Orchestra World* published an article in the spring of 1945 in which the writer pretended to be trying to interview His Majesty the King while the two jesters (meaning the other two members of the trio, Moore and Miller) kept popping up.

Playing the Trocadero in Hollywood and appearing in the picture *Stork Club* (with guest appearances by stars such as Bing Crosby and Bob Hope), for which the trio was paid $12,000, being on Bing Crosby's and Frank Sinatra's shows, appearing in the slapstick comedy *See My Lawyer* at Universal, making *Breakfast in Hollywood,* another feature film and being paid over $13,000 for it, it all meant that Madame Fortune was in a good mood and things were looking up in every way, including financially. In addition, it meant that Nat was overcoming a lot of his shyness. "For a long time I couldn't look at audiences when I performed..." Now he was on his way to become a master showman.

The Coles bought a new car, and Nat began to dress more elegantly, albeit rather flamboyantly. He had taken a fancy to suits with wide lapels, and quite wild-looking ties. Nat and Nadine were invited to parties with glamorous people. People commented on his gracious personality. He never tried to take center stage socially (he remained a shy person on the inside), but at the same time he was not self-effacing: He remained happy and grateful to life for his good fortune.

Quietly and for his own soul's sake, he kept doing jazz records for little money (forty-one dollars was standard pay for a recording). He was always working—and his home life suffered.

He went to Chicago, and his trio took time to go to his father's church and play at a benefit. The newspapers marvelled at this musical sensation who had not lost touch with his roots, his family. He was generous with them as with friends around him. He was making more money than he had ever made in his life, and he was enjoying all of it. He was generous toward his wife Nadine as well, but only with money and material things. Not with himself, not with his time. His music was a demanding mistress.

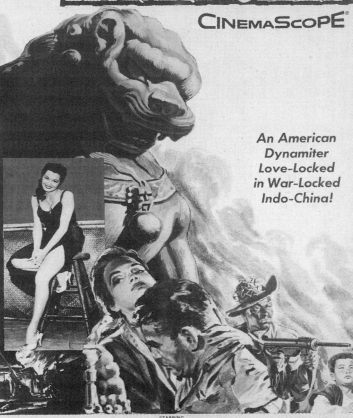

SAMUEL FULLER'S **china gate**

CINEMASCOPE®

An American Dynamiter Love-Locked in War-Locked Indo-China!

STARRING

...NE BARRY · ANGIE DICKINSON · NAT "KING" CO...

(AS BROCK) (AS LUCKY LEGS) (HIS FIRST DRAMATIC ROLE...

FEATURING

PAUL DUBOV · LEE VAN CLEEF · GEORGE GIVOT · GERALD MILTON · NEYLE MORROW · MARCEL DALIO · MAURICE MARSAC
WARREN HSIEH · PAUL BUSCH · SASHA HARDEN · JAMES HONG · WILLIAM SOO HOO · WALTER SOO HOO · WEAVER LEVY

WRITTEN, PRODUCED AND DIRECTED BY **SAMUEL FULLER** — A GLOBE ENTERPRISES PRODUCTION
Released by 20th CENTURY FOX

Chapter Six

I'm In The Mood For Love

(recorded in 1946)

Nat was close to thirty years old, Nadine was close to forty, there were no children—and the marriage was empty. Nadine had stopped traveling with him and was not around when the trio went on the road and then to Club Zanzibar in New York in 1946, where they were to substitute for the Mills Brothers who had been forced to cancel an engagement.

At the Zanzibar he saw for the first time a young attractive singer named Maria Ellington. He had come up from backstage and, seeing her from the back, was heard exclaiming, "Who is that?" following it with "Wow!

"His first dramatic role" proclaimed the posters for China Gate, in which Cole played one of a small band of foreign legionnaires trying to find a secret communist munitions supply.

If she looks as good from the front. . ."

She was tall, she had a lovely singing voice and a gorgeous face, she was intelligent and full of life. "I've never seen a black woman who spoke so well, who dressed so well, who carried herself the way she did," he told a friend.

Before long, it happened: Nat King Cole was falling in love. Deeply and completely.

Maria was not a Cole fan when they met, although her sister was, and she was to discover that so were scores of other people. Actually, when she heard that the King Cole Trio was coming in from California to replace the Mills Brothers, she asked, "Who are they?"

Then she met him and, after some initial resistance on her part, it was clear that Nat King Cole and Maria Ellington were strongly drawn to each other. He gave her tickets to the Joe Louis-Billy Conn fight (at fifty dollars a ticket, it was an impressively generous gift), he took her to the horse races, he drove her home after performances, he sent champagne to her dressing room. Indeed, the well-behaved "Boy Scout" of the music business was madly smitten.

The woman who set his heart on fire was born as Marie Antoinette Hawkins in Boston, Massachusetts, on August 1, 1922, which made her three years younger than Nat. Her mother died in childbirth a couple of years after her birth. When her father, a mail carrier, had trouble raising his three little girls on his own, his sister, Dr. Charlotte Hawkins Brown, a highly educated woman with several college degrees (and she being the granddaughter of a slave) brought the children to her own private school in Sedalia, North Carolina, the Palmer Memorial Institute, which she had started in 1902 at age nineteen (twenty years before women could vote). This meant that Maria received an excellent education including learning to speak beautifully and behave charmingly. After all, her intelligent and strict Aunt Lottie had even written an etiquette book called *The Correct Thing*. Hers was an unusual childhood for a black girl at the time—her aunt had a maid, a telephone, important guests in her home such as Eleanor Roosevelt and the poet Langston Hughes. Nevertheless, she and her aunt could not go to the fine hotels and restaurants in the area, because of their skin color. . .

Maria went on to Boston Clerical College. She wanted to sing, but her aunt despised show business and didn't think that was a proper place for "a nice girl." Having inherited her aunt's determination, Maria took her degree and then managed to get jobs with different bands, including Duke Ellington (she was one of three or four female singers). The two were not related in spite of having the same last name. She had been calling herself Marie Winter as she started singing, but then married a serviceman, Neal Ellington, a member of the legendary black 332nd Fighter Group. He was killed in an accident during a routine training flight at the end of 1945.

Shortly before she met Nat Cole, she had quit Ellington's band and was working at the Club Zanzibar as a solo singer, with two songs ("Personality" and "Come Rain or Come Shine") per show. Both her singing and her aristocratic looks and carriage impressed the customers.

Being in love created a conflict since Nat was a married man, and one who took his commitments seriously. For a while, it helped that his manager Carlos Gastel kept the trio enormously busy; they traveled all over the country, often being guaranteed $5,000 per show. In the summer of 1946 they replaced Bing Crosby, on whose show they had been guests several times. Crosby and Cole were good friends and were exceptionally good together on a stage, making light-hearted fun of each other.

The trio kept going back to New York to appear on "The Kraft Music Hall" broadcasts, which meant that the romance between Maria and Nat had opportunities to develop and blossom. Nadine remained on the West Coast, and he did go to see her in August of 1946, but had to return to New York almost immediately to record a new song.

Singer Mel Tormé and Bob Wells had written "The Christmas Song," and everybody agreed that Nat should record it with strings and a studio orchestra rather than just with his trio. It was Maria's idea that Nat should get up from the piano bench to sing (he was playing the piano himself)—he resisted a little but, because Maria had suggested it and he trusted her implicitly, he did it.

In December he was recording his first "Metronome All-Stars Record" with Charlie Shavers on trumpet, Johnny Hodges on alto saxophone, Coleman Hawkins on tenor saxophone, fabulous Buddy Rich on drums, Harry Carney on baritone saxophone, Eddie Safranski on bass, Bob Ahern on guitar, singer June Christy from Stan Kenton's band, and Frank Sinatra—Cole and Sinatra would soon be vying with each other about the place as the country's most popular male singer. Meanwhile his "The Christmas Song" recording

Nat Cole enjoyed stretching his dramatic imagination by acting but always returned to the concert stage and the recording

*tudio. In the latter he was in charge; in the movie studios he
ad to wait until called.*

stayed on top of all the charts all through the Christmas season and long after.

This was followed by a string of other Cole songs (some with his trio, others with strings) all becoming immensely popular: "Route 66," "You Call It Madness," "I Love You for Sentimental Reasons". . .

At the end of 1946 he had begun doing the radio show, "The Wildroot Cream Oil Show," which lasted until the beginning of 1949, airing every Saturday afternoon. His soothing tender voice was quite addictive, as evidenced by eager radio listeners.

The newspapers kept praising their new favorite singer, most keeping tactfully quiet about his romance with Maria. Nat was much loved by the press since he did not have a huge ego, was treating everyone courteously, and behaved discreetly in his love affair with the spirited young beauty.

Some friends kept advising him to break off the affair. There were those who found Maria snobbish due to her privileged background and excellent schooling. But Nat did not listen to any of them.

Even Oscar Moore and Johnny Miller, his long-time buddies and fellow musicians, were unhappy since Maria had disrupted their closeness and equal footing with Nat. She was very clear about Nat emerging as the absolute star of the group, which might have been another reason for their unhappiness. Nat himself, being naturally modest, was minimizing the difference, but Maria basically saw Moore and Miller as back-up musicians, although superb such, a position that they felt did not make it possible for them to grow and develop musically. Nat might have been more aware of this than he let on because in early 1947 he instigated a concert tour with "more serious music." Although in actuality, the concert was divided into three parts with pop and vocals in the first and last section and the serious instrumental part in the middle.

Maria's family and friends were shocked, as they realized that the relationship between her and Nat was serious. They took a dim view of her being involved with a married man—and a musician to boot!

Nat's family felt strong loyalty toward Nadine, and it would take them a while to adjust to the new situation. Once they got to know Maria, they accepted her fully, however.

The audience kept loving him. So did other artists, recognizing a purity and a joy in him that is found in those who are *compelled* to communicate something to their audiences. Orson Welles and Duke Ellington were a couple of artists who felt a strong kinship with Nat. The pianist Oscar Peterson, who would become the most acclaimed jazz pianist in the world, said in several interviews later on that he and his trio learned most from Cole (Peterson even sounded like him when he sang which he did only occasionally).

Nat knew that he had to do something to straighten up and fly right in his private life and the something was a divorce from Nadine. His manager, Gastel, warned him that it would cost plenty. "It doesn't matter," said Nat. "Do you love this woman $60,000 dollars worth?" asked Gastel. "I do," answered Nat.

And Nadine? For a long time she had suspected nothing since the affair was happening on the East Coast. Somebody might finally have told her, because she took a train to New York some time in 1946. When she and Nat met, he told her the truth. She returned to Los Angeles almost immediately. If it was hard on her, she never let on but said only, "I took it pretty well. After all, he had been on the road so much during our marriage."

He gave her their newly bought house free and clear and agreed to pay her at least a hundred dollars per week for ten years or until she remarried. He left her one life insurance policy as well. The two remained on friendly terms after the divorce. They were two people who respected and liked each other even if their marriage had broken up. She went to hear him in clubs sometimes—he would send her a warm note on special days. Neither developed a habit of speaking ill of the other. She retained the name Coles (his real name) for the rest of her life, which she largely devoted to working with blind and handicapped persons.

He never stopped worrying about Nadine's welfare, but his love for Maria was strong. The two women were much alike in some ways and each other's opposites in others.

One must remember that in the '40s, divorce was far from as common as today, and many were critical of men who left their wives for other women. It helped that there were no scandals surrounding this particular divorce. Maria and Nat did live together as soon as he was legally separated, but they were not obvious about it.

Maria's influence was soon noticed—Nat's speech became more polished, his diction more perfect, he dressed more stylishly (narrower lapels) in well-tailored suits. Nat Cole was interested in clothes—which makes sense since he was generally a visual person—but his taste had leaned toward flashy clothes, until Maria came and guided him in the direction of a more subdued and elegant look. She encouraged his wearing hats and during the years he acquired quite a collection, having always admired people such as Rex Harrison and Tony Martin who wore hats, almost like a trademark. Even his skin improved. She had noticed that the stage makeup along with his diet had created some problems and made him take time to clean his face thoroughly after each performance after which he was to use plenty of cold water to close the pores. Maria looked after him in big things as well as small things; his career, his looks, his well-being in every way were important to her.

His personal valet, also his good friend and confidante, a bright, loyal man named Baldwin Tavares, called Sparky by all, used to say, "A good man is hard to find. A good woman is a miracle."

Nat was happier and more confident, as his personal life became more fulfilling. "He was a good man and easy to live with if a woman was not jealous of his work," says one friend from those days, pointing out that he was a Pisces (musicians tended to talk a lot about astrology then). "He was a typical Pisces. He didn't like arguments and tension. He didn't like to get upset and seldom did. But when necessary he could make you listen to him."

Smiling, smoking, relaxed, popular. . . Nat King Cole was
liked by just about everyone who come into contact with him.
Here he takes a work break along with actor Gene Barry.

Chapter Seven

Magic
Moments
(recorded in November 1961)

The divorce became final in 1948, which turned out to be quite a year for Nat King Cole.

First, elaborate wedding plans were under way.

Some friends wanted to hold the wedding reception at a fashionable hotel in midtown New York, but the hotel didn't want a party for a black entertainer there, famous or not. There was still a strong color line at the hotels in New York (when Nat sang at one of them, he usually stayed in a hotel in Harlem; the first non-Harlem hotel to accept him and other

Sarah Vaughan attended Nat and Maria's wedding. She and Nat toured with "The Big Show" in 1953, and she remained Natalie Cole's favorite throughout the years.

blacks seems to have been the Capitol).

As the civil rights movement was slowly, very slowly, gaining momentum, some thought that Nat King Cole's wedding could be a great occasion to combine celebrity guests of all colors and religions. His appeal was equally strong among white audiences as among black. (Even stronger, some insisted.)

The actual ceremony took place at the Abyssinian Baptist Church in Harlem, and the famous Reverend Adam Clayton Powell, Jr., also a Democratic congressman from New York (who was married to Hazel Scott, a popular jazz pianist and one of Maria's closest friends), officiated. The date was March 28, 1948, a cold and clear Easter Sunday. The bride wore a blue off-shoulder satin gown and carried a bouquet of white roses.

The wedding was preceded by a bachelor party that nearly wrecked the wedding! It was held at Al and Dick's on West Fifty-Fourth Street and lasted until the wee hours of morning. Maria did not approve, since she had been told what went on at such stag parties. Nat, who normally drank moderately if at all, got quite drunk. Somehow, the couple ironed out their differences hours before they pronounced their marriage vows.

About three thousand people attended the

church ceremony. *Life* and *Look* covered the wedding prominently, and *The New York Times* took notice as well.

Sarah Vaughan, Bill "Bojangles" Robinson and a great number of other celebrities attended. Eddie Cole was Nat's best man, Maria's sister Charlotte was matron of honor, her other sister Carol was a bridesmaid and Carol's little daughter, also named Carol, was a flower girl.

The lavish reception had been set at the new Belmont Plaza Hotel (on Lexington Avenue in the East Forties). Its manager, who had been told that there would be more white guests than black, saw all the black folks coming in (they were in the majority) and nearly had conniptions.

Nat and Maria set out on a honeymoon in Mexico City, where there was a one minute earthquake during their stay, and Acapulco, then still a sleepy little seaport. *Ebony* sent a photographer to Mexico to take pictures.

A great gift was a telegram telling them about the record "Nature Boy" having become the number one hit in the United States.

After a week Nat had to return and resume his successful tour. Nat's hometown paper for the black community, the *Chicago Defender,* named his trio as the best small combo and

The Nat King Cole Show, ran for a total of sixty weeks on NBC. He made several movies, toured extensively, including in

Europe, Australia and Latin America; his work schedule was at times unbelievable. But he did not let the strain show...

Nat as the best pianist in the country. He won
other polls, and made his second "Metronome
All-Stars Record" together with another
struggling young musician, Dizzy Gillespie.

Due to all the traveling, the newly-marrieds
lived in suitcases for a couple of years. There
were always the problems of segregation,
especially in some places, and a network of
black families offered the Coles a place to stay
to save them from the humiliation of "sorry,
no blacks" at the hotel. Even if it wasn't
always said in so many words.

Wanting a permanent base, they went house
hunting in Los Angeles and found an enormous brick Tudor mansion, complete with
sweeping staircase and ornate chandelier, at
401 South Muirfield Road in Hancock Park,
an exclusive section of Los Angeles. In this
area lived rich white people. No blacks. It has
been said that the purchase of the house was
handled by a middle person, possibly the sister
of Nat's (white) manager.

The news of the Coles having bought the
house caused an uproar. Neighbors tried to
prohibit them from moving in; one reported-
ly offered to buy it back for about $110,000
(the purchase price was $85,000); rocks were
thrown on the lawn, a shot might have been
fired through a window though Nat felt this

was a mistake. Unfortunately the police report regarding this has been destroyed. Cole, remaining calm throughout, offered to meet with his neighbors to allay their fears. "I would like to meet all my new neighbors and explain the situation to them. My bride and I like this house. We can afford it. And we would like to make it our home."

The lawyer representing the aggressive opponents told him, "Mr. Cole, I want you to understand our position. We don't want any undesirable people coming into the neighborhood, you know."

"Neither do I," replied Nat. "If I see anybody undesirable coming in, I'll be the first to complain."

(Later on, many of the residents who once were up in arms, were bragging about having Nat King Cole for a neighbor.)

They moved in, and Maria set about decorating. Their home became a showcase with a 13 foot long floor-to-ceiling mirror and an eight-feet custom-built sofa in the living room, a white fireplace in the bedroom with white and pink antique satin covering chairs and the king-size bed's headboard.

Tragedy struck when Maria's younger sister Carol, who had been widowed about a year and a half earlier, died of tuberculosis. Nat and

Prepare well and give your total concentration to what you are doing, would be Cole's advice to aspiring actors. Filming

movies such as China Gate *took place under less than luxurious circumstances, the hours were long—and he loved it!*

Maria adopted her little girl Carol, who was born on October 17, 1944. They called her "Cookie" and, while mourning and missing Carol, delighted in their new role as parents, a role they had won over Maria's Aunt Lottie, who had wanted the child but who had met a stubbornness matching her own in the usually so gentle and easygoing Nat.

But they had little time to enjoy their home and new family, as Nat was touring constantly, his success growing in leaps and bounds. The telephone kept ringing. Every songwriter in town wanted Nat Cole to try out his song, certain that he could make any song a success by singing it in his heartfelt manner. "Nature Boy" remained a big hit, often requested, and it was followed by "Put 'Em in a Box, Tie it with a Ribbon," "Don't Blame Me," and "Little Girl." Every December his "The Christmas Song" was greeted with acclamation and joy.

The story of how "Nature Boy" came to Nat is worth recalling. Being constantly besieged by songwriters wherever he went, some even following him into the men's room in restaurants, Nat and his entourage did what they could to avoid those of amateur status. But one time when the trio was performing at a Los Angeles theater, an insistent young man with long reddish hair and unconventional clothes brought a song on a soiled sheet of music, saying that Johnny Mercer at Capitol had suggested he take it to Nat Cole. The song was called "Nature Boy Suite." The man gave his name as Eden Ahbez.

Nat looked at the song some days later and liked something about it. After the Second World War, there were strong pro-Jewish sentiments, and he had been looking for a song that somehow expressed this.

Some time passed, and at another concert Nat's manager Carlos Gastel suggested that he try out "that Jewish-sounding song." He did. Irving Berlin who was in the house asked to buy the song immediately after the trio had finished the set. Nat explained that he didn't know where the strange Eden Ahbez could be found. His curiosity piqued, he asked his people to try to find Eden. No luck. Cole continued to sing the song in live performances, and the reactions were indeed positive. He also included the song, rather casually, in a recording session at Capitol. Now both his producer and he wanted to find the author of it.

They did find him, living in a garden or somewhere outdoors (under the L in the Hollywood sign, some reports say) with a pregnant wife, practicing yoga, eating fruits and nuts, and communing with the universe. He

John Drew Barrymore and Julie London, as two newlyweds, greet Anna Kashfi and Nat King Cole in the 1959 film, Night of the Quarter Moon, also released under the title Flesh and

*the Flame. How does a man in San Francisco's high society
in the 1950s handle the discovery that his bride is a quarter
black? Nat's part of the uncle was another foray into drama.*

had been roaming around the country for years before he settled in California and took his name, which he wrote without capitals, believing that no human being rated capitals (these he reserved for words such as Life, Love, Nature, Peace, Energy. . .). In other words, a true hippie quite a while before the flower children of the 1960s.

Thinking it over, Capitol felt the song's lyrics were too subtle, and it was not included in the recording, after all. A few months later, Nat did record it in New York with a full orchestra, and Capitol paid *eden ahbez* the rather odd sum he requested as an advance (the sum was never revealed). It was presented with "Lost April" on the reverse side. The first time it was broadcast on WNEW radio station, the disc jockey was besieged with phone calls, and for the next several weeks the song was airing at least ten times a day with calls from excited listeners pouring in. Nat was pleased that a black guy singing about universal love could reach so many, across racial and other barriers.

While jazz remained his big love, it was the ballads, the pop songs and the novelty stuff that brought in the money. Now and then he managed to sneak in a jazz tune, such as "Sweet Georgia Brown."

The trio underwent some changes. Oscar Moore left, saying he was "tired of constantly being on the road," and he was replaced by Irving Ashby, born in 1920. There were some disagreements about money and Oscar did sue Nat; they settled out of court. Some blamed Maria Cole for rising tensions having to do with finances and with breaking up the ensemble feeling of the group. It seems that she did take over the reins, and equally true that she was seeing her husband as the undisputed leader, the real star. She was right, of course, and the fact that Nat reached such heights is undoubtedly to a great extent due to her careful, detailed planning. He was drawn to her strength (she was a Leo); she was attracted to his gentleness (he was a Pisces). He was much more gullible than she, always seeing the good in people.

Good reviews continued as critics found that "the trio has perfected a style which blends sophisticated harmonies with a clean, agile solo technique and poignant ensemble variations." Which simply meant that they played great together and each one did very well on his own. Another reviewer said, "Outstanding among Nat's performance attributes are the creation of a rhythmic pulse so dominant that it is recreated in the feelings of the listener."

Nat appreciated the good words but had not particularly high opinions of critics; he admired those who were *doing something* more than those who were *commenting* on the doings of others; his heart was with those who took risks.

He valued more the praise from his peers. As when Billy Eckstine said, "This guy did what Louis Armstrong did: He took a style and made a voice of it."

Then Johnny Miller left the trio. His wife was ill, and he did not want to be away from her for months on end. Ever energetic and innovative, Nat thought of blending strings into his trio. "Everybody who has a creative mind should keep finding new ways of doing things," he said. Then he abandoned the idea of strings and put a bongo and conga player into the group instead.

He still did not see himself as a singer. "I sing because the public buys it."

The famous Ciro's on the Sunset Strip booked the trio, and on opening night a crowd including an Egyptian prince and Hollywood actors (such as Ronald Reagan) applauded enthusiastically. Did that mean that blacks were becoming accepted by the white world? Not at all. During the same engagement at Ciro's, it happened that a couple of friends of his, a black gospel singer and a black athlete, made reservations, only to be met by the manager who claimed that the club was filled up. No seats, in spite of reservations. When Nat heard about this, he told them, "The job doesn't mean so much to me that my people have to be insulted when they come to hear us play." He offered to be a witness for his friends if they decided to sue the club.

Chapter Eight

Nobody Knows The Trouble I've Seen

(recorded in September 1958)

Cole and Capitol grew together in an arrangement that was mutually beneficial. It has been estimated that Nat Cole's annual gross sales for Capitol came close to two and a half million dollars during his first ten years with the company. Wallichs of Capitol praised him as "our most consistent solo artist," saying that any song sung by Cole had an eighty percent chance of becoming a hit.

Nat was becoming rich, never earning less than a quarter of a million per year and sometimes considerably more. At the time, half a million sales made a record a sensational

Nat Cole called Lena Horne "a lady with the courage of her convictions which spells a real lady." Although largely apolitical, he stood by her during the McCarthy era.

hit—and several of Nat Cole's sold over a million each; a couple of them closer to two million copies.

According to all reports, he remained "a thoroughly nice human being," who awakened loyalty in those who worked for him. He liked things to be perfect, to run smoothly, but he did not have an immense ego and no desire to put others down. He was what some term a man's man, who was appreciated by women. He was elegant, "a lovely guy," extremely courteous toward all, not the least the ladies. "One of the most gentlemanly, kindest, most helpful persons I have ever known," said Jack Constanzo, the white conga player.

He did get upset occasionally, usually for good reasons, as when he came to Las Vegas and discovered the obvious racial barriers. In spite of great popularity and glowing reviews, blacks, including him, were not welcome in the casinos, for instance. Think of it for a moment—the star of the show (this was the Thunderbird) could not enter the hotel gambling casino nor any other part of the hotel except for a small room adjoining the kitchen! He swore he wouldn't go back until things changed. They did pretty quickly after that (the casino owners realized his drawing power), and he was definitely one of the artists responsible for breaking down racial barriers in that gambling paradise. Although he developed a good relationship with the Sands, he would never play the Sahara, a hotel that had wanted him to perform. Deciding to check out the place, he went over with some friends and was stopped by a security guard. Embarrassed and angry, he swore he would never play the Sahara, and he never did. At the Desert Inn, he was treated royally but soon realized that this treatment was due to him being a celebrity and did not extend to other blacks. So he would not accept any Desert Inn dates either.

He was tired of constantly encountering racism in the South and in the North, both the overt kind and the more subtle variety.

Many women of any color fawned over the impeccably elegant Nat with the sparkling eyes and took to calling him "The Black Panther." His trusted valet Sparky and his manager Carlos Gastel had to protect him from overly avid female admirers. A rule, possibly established by Maria, forbade any females to visit with Nat in his dressing room. He would greet them, standing in the doorway, and even meet them for drinks along with his manager and Sparky, but he never entertained any women in his dressing room. Thereby there was no food for scandal.

In *Night of the Quarter Moon*, Julie London marries a wealthy man, played by John Drew Barrymore. (At the right is the great

Billy Daniels, who had a small role in the film.) Then her dear dark-skinned uncle (Nat King Cole) arrives...

Didn't anybody criticize him? Of course there were critics, even among blacks. Nat was criticized for hiring the white bongo player, Jack Constanzo, who had been a member of Stan Kenton's band. "Best man for the job," was Nat's calm response always. He didn't regret his decision nor attempt to change it, even when segregation reared its ugly head as when Constanzo was forced to stay in a separate hotel in some places—in others he was not even permitted to play with the group. A couple of times he was not allowed on stage for safety reasons because threats about "the white boy" had been received.

Again, Nat's reasons for adding a bongo player to his group was his constant drive to refresh and renew the sound and the rhythms. "The change gives us a progressive feeling. . . A lot of the tension the bass and I used to feel is gone now because the bongo and conga drums give the rhythm we were supposed to give. That leaves us free to do much more."

Traveling as an integrated group could have been more problematic than it was, had it not been for the black members keeping up the frequent practice of staying in private homes.

In 1950, Nat brought a $62,000 suit against an Illinois hotel for refusing him a room (in

June of that year) because of his race. The case came up in September of 1951, and he testified that he was treated "like a little fly that might be in the way" when he tried to take possession of the room he had reserved. After his testimony, he left before the verdict in order to appear at a cancer benefit in New York. He won the suit.

Those were some of the frustrations but being on the road had its bright spots. Whenever the group met up with other musicians on the road, such as Lionel Hampton, a jam session could last all night.

Nat's constant travel companions were his two dogs, the boxers Mr. Cole and Mr. Pep. And nearly always Maria was by his side, even taking her chance to perform during a visit to Boston, her hometown. However, Nat was of the opinion that one career in the family was enough so she remained mainly his "Queen," looking every inch the part, often wearing a tiara as she went to club openings. Then, in 1949, while on the road with him as he was doing a string of one-nighters, she discovered she was pregnant. Nat was dizzy with delight.

The group had kept changing, partly because the life on the road took its toll on the men—and their marriages. Now the steady members were the bassist Charles Harris and

Nat King Cole not only acted but sang and played the piano in the then controversial love story Night of the Quarter Moon

with Julie London, John Drew Barrymore, Anna Kashfi, Dean Jones, and Agnes Moorehead.

John Collins, who had known Nat from high school, on guitar.

Nat was recording more and more—"Mona Lisa" became a huge hit along with others, including some of the whimsical ones such as "Ke Mo Ky Mo," "The Frim Fram Sauce," and "Oh Kickeroonie"—the latter two for his *Nat Cole for Kids* album. And then there was "Unforgettable."

A bigger thrill to him than all his success was that on February 6, 1950—shortly before "Mona Lisa" was released—Maria gave birth to a little girl named Natalie Maria, soon called "Sweetie" by her adoring dad and her excited big sister "Cookie," now five and a half. Nat had made sure that he only took engagements in Los Angeles the weeks before the birth of Natalie. He wasn't going to miss her entrance on the stage of the world, during which he paced nervously, more jittery than at any performance. He was in his early thirties and finally a biological father, something he had wanted and dreamt of for many years.

Even with Natalie an infant, Maria kept going on the road with her husband, not wanting to be separated from him for long times. She had learned her lesson from his first wife who stayed at home while he roamed the nation—after all, that's how she, Maria, met and fell in love with him. She also felt that he needed her, not the least for a lot of practical matters. Besides, she was seriously considering returning to her own singing career. This time she received all assistance from Nat and made a few recordings. (He might have been so giddily happy about the child that he would do just about anything to make his wife happy.) But she became pregnant almost immediately again, although she miscarried when Natalie was nine months old.

Since Maria did not stay home, her sister Charlotte, who worked as Nat's personal secretary, supervised home and children when the Coles were on the road.

One day she opened the door to find grimfaced men from the Internal Revenue Service on the threshold. They were there to seize the house for back taxes! Shocked, Charlotte ran to the phone.

Nat, who was in Philadelphia, canceled his tour and flew with Maria back to Los Angeles, where big signs informed the surrounding world that the Coles would lose their house. Their cars had already been seized. Later the tax people would come to take household effects and nearly took the piano as well until Maria's sister in no uncertain words pointed out that the piano was how Nat Cole made his living.

The New York Times wrote on March 14, 1951:

"The Collector of Internal Revenue ordered the $85,000 home of Nat (King) Cole, singer, seized and sold for nonpayment of income tax today. The collector, Robert A. Ridell, said the Negro musician owed the government $146,000 for income tax in 1947, 1948 and 1949. He ordered the seizure under a 100-year-old law and said the house might be sold within twenty days."

Even with his enormous earning power, Nat did not have cash on hand. Maria's aunt gave them $20,000 right away to keep the tax men at bay, all the earlier friction between her and Nat having melted away.

A good accountant named Phil Braunstein started taking over the affairs. He suspected and probably rightly so that some of the IRS agents did not think a black family belonged in the exclusive part of town. (Why did the IRS go after the house directly; why not attach his salary and royalties from his recordings?) Braunstein used his clout and informed the agents that if a settlement was not drawn up right away, he would make a legal issue out of the matter.

It might be worth noting the general context of Nat Cole's tax problems. This was the time of the infamous McCarthy hearings, and many famous blacks, Jews, and other people who might be suspected of leaning to the left politically, found themselves under the magnifying glass of governmental agencies. Several black entertainers had trouble at this time. Lena Horne was blacklisted for having been associated with controversial causes. Paul Robeson was, of course, a particular target. Nat had avoided controversy, but he did not cut people out of his life because they were in trouble. Lena Horne remained a close friend, as did Paul Robeson, whom he went to visit in England. Maintaining friendships with "suspect" people was at the time enough for somebody to be scrutinized.

In his case, he probably did owe what the government said he did—it's the matter of recovery one might question. He earned big money, and he spent big money. There were agents and managers, valets and maids, travel and housing and tips; the mortgage was large, he was generous toward Maria and toward friends. Never overly concerned about money, he was eager to help those who were less fortunate than he was. He was not working for the money but for the sheer joy of it, delighted to be able to provide for those he loved. "I learned the hard way about money," he said in an interview in *Ebony*. "I had my little follies. I was, what you might say, conned out of a lot of money, and I gave a lot of it away. But when I got in that trouble, I got the message. All of us get the message, sooner or later. If you get it before it's too late or before you're too old, you'll pull through all right."

Between Braunstein, manager Carlos Gastel and Capitol Records a deal was worked out. Capitol wrote out a check for $30,000 to be paid at once. That along with the $20,000 check from Maria's Aunt Lottie meant that the debt was reduced by $50,000 immediately; Capitol further agreed to pay the IRS $30,000 directly every year for the next four years.

The Coles got their Cadillac back, and the seizure signs were taken off their house.

Though the times were trying and Nat had trouble sleeping, he never blamed anyone— not his managers nor his accountants. "It was all my fault," he said.

Both the Coles handled the strain under which they lived for a number of years with elegance.

Showmanship was the key word, professionally and privately for Nat Cole. He emphasized that it was not just the sound that counted—things had to look right as well. He paid lots of attention to how he and his musicians were lighted on stage, and to how they were dressed, knowing that the over-all atmosphere was of immense importance. "Make it look good and it will sound twice as good to the average guy because everything is visual to the public."

He knew an audience didn't care if the artist was tired or had tax problems or any other problems. They came to be entertained, and the entertainer entertains, whatever else is happening.

He gave plenty of credit to Maria. He told an *Ebony* reporter that she was "the chancellor of my exchequer who has balanced my budget." He said she had given him more confidence and taught him to be more aggressive in dealings with club managers. "Commercially, musically, and psychologically, I am a much-improved man," he said. "I have a greater urge for wholesome hobbies like golf and photography and spend more time at them. I hate to appear immodest, but marrying Maria was a major stroke of genius. I have gained more than I can say."

Chapter Nine

Ebony Rhapsody

(recorded in November 1961)

The hits kept coming: "Too Young" (the number one song of 1951 on jukeboxes, in record sales and in radio plays), "Red Sails in the Sunset," "Because of Rain" and so on. Also, Nat and his trio worked steadily at the Paramount in New York, at the Thunderbird in Las Vegas, at the Fairmont in San Francisco, at Ciro's in Los Angeles.

Some complained that he had left jazz too far behind and become too commercial, but one writer pointed out, "The cry we've heard around is that Cole is commercial, which is always aimed at anyone who becomes suc-

Nat King Cole and Johnnie Ray rehearse before the start of Cole's weekly television show.

cessful."

Nat shrugged whenever a critic blasted him, "Critics don't buy records; they get them for free."

He knew that what they meant was that he did more and more singing and less and less instrumentals. The early established fact remained that the public liked his singing style and the kinds of songs he sang better than the jazz music he so enjoyed playing. Ballads had increased in popularity immensely. "Luckily for me, they're the songs I do best," said Nat.

He did cut down on his performing schedule somewhat in order to spend more time with his family. Cookie and Sweetie were dear to him, and he didn't want them growing up with him always absent.

The Sands in Las Vegas increased his salary, and he signed a contract for a three-week stretch each year for three years at $12,500 a week, beginning in January 1954.

Again, it was the 1950s and racial prejudice was alive and sick. Some commented that if he only were white, he would be bigger than anyone. He was famous and rich (well, at least he had the potential in spite of IRS), but he kept running into that invisible (and sometimes highly visible) barrier of color, and kept being frustrated by the never-ending, dehumanizing effects of racism.

"It makes me sick that a man's skin seems so much more important than his heart and his mind and his soul," he said.

He began having stomach pains but largely ignored these, thinking they were mainly symptoms of nerves and sometimes of frustration.

In 1953 he went on a tour with the Big Show with arranger and orchestra leader Billy May. Sarah Vaughan was one of the singers. The tour was going well; Billy May, as others before and after, found Nat extremely easy to work with.

But on Easter Sunday, April 5, 1953, Nat had felt strong stomach pains during a performance in a television studio. Sparky helped him out of the studio to take a taxi back to the Warwick Hotel where they were staying. It took quite a while to catch a taxi since many cab drivers kept on driving when seeing a black potential customer. That night Nat had a concert at Carnegie Hall, and he was not going to miss it.

A music publisher, Ivan Mogull, stopped by the hotel, realized that Nat was very ill and talked him into letting a doctor see him before the performance. The doctor told Nat that he had bleeding ulcers. Still, Nat went on stage

36-18

The Nat "King" Cole Musical Story (1955) told the tale of
Cole's early life, his musical genius becoming evident, his rise

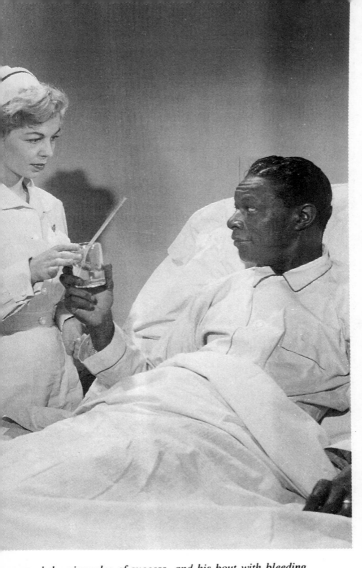

*toward the pinnacles of success, and his bout with bleeding
ulcer which brought him low for a while. Nat played himself.*

and performed at the 8:30 show but had to cancel the midnight show; he was rushed to the hospital where he underwent surgery.

Forced to recuperate for several months— and even being forbidden to smoke for a while, a tough thing for a heavy smoker—he was restless. Performing was his life, even if his life as an artist often brought about such pressures and anxiety that he, although outwardly seeming calm and collected, chain-smoked and bit his fingernails to the quick.

Some friends say that this forced time of rest made him more quiet and introspective than before.

Meanwhile his recordings kept rising to the top of the charts, and he could hardly turn on the radio without hearing himself sing.

The best part about this period was the time he had to spend with Cookie and Sweetie. He was a devoted, sometimes overly generous father. He even took them into a studio to record, getting a kick out of how Sweetie (Natalie) tended to imitate him, singing "Walking My Baby Back Home" with gusto.

In a sea of divorces all around them, the Coles stood out as an amazingly solid couple. Show business and marriage do not always blend well. The lifestyle of a musician, who is by necessity a night person, is often in strong conflict with any semblance of family life. But Nat and Maria, who must have had their share of disagreements and tensions, showed a united front toward all, and evidenced loyalty and respect toward each other. By now, they were talking more and more about adopting a baby boy.

As 1954 rolled in, Nat was back on the road again.

He was now the highest paid entertainer at the Sands in Las Vegas, and performed regularly at the Copacabana in New York, the Coconut Grove in Los Angeles, and the Chez Paree in Chicago.

Success remained his companion.

"Darling, Je Vous Aime Beaucoup," he sang with that voice that reached into people's hearts and souls. Nobody else sounded like Nat King Cole.

In Las Vegas or Lake Tahoe, he would sometimes bump into his good friend Sammy Davis Jr., and the two would go out for a rollicking time after respective performances, with plenty of gambling, laughing, and joke-telling.

In 1954 the Coles went to France where he played at the Palais du Chaillot. The French loved him, calling him "an artist, a thorough musician." Their only complaint was that he didn't play the piano more.

They continued on to England. The first time there, in 1950, his reception had been somewhat lukewarm; now he was known (partly due to the introduction of jukeboxes, partly because people had heard him on the radio), so restaurant orchestras frequently began playing one of his tunes whenever Nat and Maria entered. His concerts at the Palladium, where he performed with his own trio, backed up by a British orchestra, were sold out.

His artistry enchanted the British, as did his personality. "He doesn't act like a big shot," was an often-heard comment. The only complaint voiced by the audiences was that the teenagers in the galleries tended to scream so loud when he started a song that part of it was lost. Nat was both surprised and a little embarrassed by this show of affection. "It's probably some form of mob psychology," he tried to explain, well aware that in the United States such demonstrations only happened to white performers such as Frank Sinatra and Johnnie Ray.

In Scotland they called Nat Cole "that sleek black Prince of Song." After each performance, lots of young ladies waited outside the stage door. They found the man with the dusky voice mysterious and exotic.

On to Ireland where several hundred people gathered outside his window. "I'd lean out the window and sing to them. And they'd sing Irish songs back at me. We'd keep it up for an hour," he told a reporter, adding, "You know, they sang much better than I do."

He was offered and took acting roles in films, had his own television show in the late '50s, produced his own stage show and tried to take it to Broadway in the '60s—and now and then he went and played pure jazz (as is evidenced on the record that he made with some of the best jazz musicians around and which became a jazz classic, "After Midnight.") Part of the inspiration for that—an undertaking he had talked about for years—was the melancholy, nostalgic mood he was in after the loss of his mother.

On February 23, 1955, at age sixty-three, his mother died of cancer. Nat and Maria had gone to Chicago to see her before her death. His father was still pastor of the First Baptist Church.

On October 5, 1955, it was Maria's turn to open in a night club act at Ciro's. Nat sent her a telegram: "If they love your act half as much as I love you then smash will be your triumph. Your Husband." He told reporters that she loved singing so much that she "was even caught

*St. Louis Blues starred Nat as W.C. Handy and featured Pearl
Bailey, Cab Calloway, Ella Fitzgerald, Mahalia Jackson. The*

cleancut young man is torn between the good girl (Ruby Dee) and the wicked city woman (Eartha Kitt).

sing-walking in her sleep." It was a thirty-minute act with blues occupying a good deal of the program, interwoven with some ballads and a humorous song, "The Wrong Mink." Having been able to take on this challenge, she seemed content to spend most of her time with her family, being their tower of strength.

In 1956, during the tour of the South with Ted Heath and his British band, there occurred the vicious attack upon him in the Birmingham Municipal Auditorium.

The attack itself was a frightening thing, but it was hitting him almost harder that his own people kept criticizing him afterwards. He believed he had behaved correctly in connection with any outburst of violent or covert racism, and it was hurting deeply when he was called an Uncle Tom. "When you've got the respect of white and colored, you can erase a lot of things . . . I can help ease the tension by gaining the respect of both races all over the country," he told reporters.

About a month after the Birmingham incident, he wrote a long letter to *Downbeat* magazine which said in part:

"To the Editor:

"I have been quite concerned over reports appearing in newspapers which purport to represent my views on Jim Crow and discrimination . . .

"First of all, I would like to say that I am, have been and will continue to be dedicated to the complete elimination of all forms of discrimination, segregation and bigotry. There is only one position in this matter and that is the right one: Full equality for all people, regardless of race, creed or religion.

"This has been my position all along, and contrary to any published reports, it remains my position. I have fought, in what I consider an effective manner, against the evil of race bigotry through the years. I had hoped that through the medium of my music I had made many new friends and changed many opinions regarding racial equality. I have always been of the opinion that by living equality, living as a full American dedicated to the democratic principle, that [I] was helping fight bigotry by example as much as the NAACP and other organizations have fought through the courts.

"I do not want to be defensive about my position. I stand on my record . . ."

Reeling from the shock of all this, he set his eye on work, steadfastly believing that's how he would make a difference. He was not a militant man. He did not involve himself in politics, he did not flirt with leftist causes as many entertainers at the time did, although he would do benefit performances for civil rights and pursue his own private battle against racism (such as segregated neighborhoods, hotels, casinos). Sometimes, according to some reports, he felt that even light-skinned blacks did not quite understand what it was to be very dark, a fact he had always lived with and which he dealt with in his own, personal way, determinedly working toward success in spite of all odds against him. Maria Cole said in her book, "Nat sincerely believed in the inherent good and kindness of man, that good did indeed eventually triumph over evil, and in the Christian ethic of turning the other cheek."

Another friend said, "He was the most unhating person I've ever known." He hated the system of injustice, but he separated the system from the person and did not hate individuals who had become victims of that system and therefore did hateful things.

Frank Sinatra and Nat King Cole were vying for the position as most popular male vocalist during the late '40s and '50s. A close friendship grew between the two men.

Chapter Ten

Around The World

(recorded in August 1957)

By now he was truly internationally famous. Actually, Nat Cole, Benny Goodman and Louis Armstrong were the musical artists most recognized all over the world.

One night he was scheduled to appear on the Ed Sullivan "Toast of the Town" show. So was Tony Martin. Sullivan asked them which one should go on first, and Martin said simply, "Nat goes first. He is the star."

Another time he was not allowed (by the sponsors) to sing a duet and appear in a skit with a female white singer.

People were talking about the impact of

Some almost forgot Cole's magic touch at the piano since his singing became enormously popular. Let it be reiterated that he was a sensational and influential jazz pianist.

television on the entertainment business, some even calling it "the evil eye" that emptied the clubs and the theaters and the nightspots as people elected to sit at home staring at a small screen. Nat, realizing the power of the medium, wanted his own television show. Nobody seemed interested but Carlos Gastel kept trying, and finally NBC showed real interest with the result that Nat was set to star in his own fifteen minute show on Monday nights at 7:30 p.m. It opened on November 5, 1956, and the reviews were fabulous. Since there were no sponsors, NBC picked up the bill for a start, hoping that sponsors would be attracted shortly.

Nat was thrilled. "I've been waging a personal campaign, aiming at a show of this kind," he told reporters. "I hit a few snags here and there but I didn't give up the fight." He hoped this would be a turning point, opening the door for black entertainers on television.

He worked with a vocal group, the quintet Botaneers, his own trio, and an orchestra with Gordon Jenkins as orchestra leader, but he was the definite focus of attention. He was keeping the format simple, feeling that too many tried for huge productions in an attempt to be different. "Simple might be a good idea. For me anyway," he said. He was aiming for the kind of spontaneity he had created in his nightclub performances.

However, no sponsors were coming forward. They were afraid that they would lose customers in the South if they sponsored him. At least that's what they said but was that their real worry? Or was it the less overt commercially deadly racism in the North? One cosmetics company stated bluntly, "Negroes cannot sell lipsticks." This infuriated Cole. "What do they think we use? Chalk? Congo paint? And what about corporations like the telephone company? A man sees a Negro on a television show. What's he going to do—call up the phone company and tell them to take out the phone?"

He did feel that the North ("where Madison Avenue is, and they run television") sometimes used the South "as a football to take some of the stain off us in the North. I have been well received in nightclubs and on records—why not TV? You don't judge entertainment on a racial basis."

The show had fine audience ratings, and NBC kept it up at a cost of $20,000 a week. (The musicians in the back-up band were working for scale; there was little money for lavish production numbers; Nat's own salary did frequently go back to cover production costs.) A company called Carter Products sponsored it for a while, the show was expanded to half an hour and moved to 10:30 p.m. on July 1, 1957. Nelson Riddle became the orchestra leader and another choral group stepped in.

A score of famous entertainers agreed to work the show for union minimum, to help Nat and NBC: Ella Fitzgerald, Peggy Lee, Tony Martin, Harry Belafonte, Bing Crosby, Sammy Davis, Jr., Louis Armstrong, and Eartha Kitt, to name a few.

August rolled around and still no sponsors. NBC had decided to replace Nat by a Western show on September 24 when, around the middle of September, there was a willing sponsor, Rheingold Beer. "This show has quality, and Cole has even outranked 'The 64,000 Question' (which was an enormously popular quiz show at the time)," said a spokesman. So Rheingold was going to sponsor the show but only in the East where they were selling their beer. Two wine companies stepped in to be the sponsors in the West. To this were added about sixteen regional sponsors.

NBC aired the show at 7:30 p.m. on Tuesdays.

The ratings (the Bible for the life of TV shows, even today) were encouraging. Many wanted to see Nat King Cole succeed—some as another step in the fight against racism, others because he was such a great entertainer, and many for both these reasons.

But the Tuesday night time slot didn't last long. NBC wanted to move Nat to Saturday nights at 7:00 p.m. "That time is for children's cowboy shows," said Carlos Gastel who knew about such things. Nat and Carlos felt it was better that he quit at this time, having run sixty weeks, than move into a slot that would mean rapidly falling ratings and what some might call failure.

Instead Carlos booked him on a tour to Australia.

In interviews, Nat was open with the reporters. "I'm leaving television because of the ad agencies," said he, adding that he felt strong restraints from somewhere. About sponsors Nat said, "(They) don't have any guts. Madison Avenue is afraid of the dark."

He did praise NBC, however. "(NBC) supported this show from the beginning. From Mr. Sarnoff on down, they tried to sell it to agencies. They could have dropped it after the first thirteen weeks. Shows that made more money than mine were dropped. [Instead] I was offered a Saturday early evening spot but decided not to take it."

A lot of people did not understand this racist play behind the scenes. All they knew

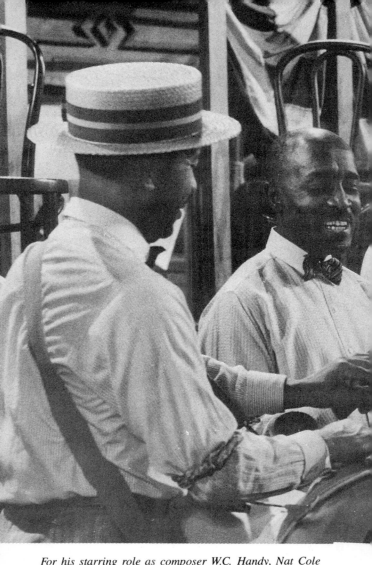

For his starring role as composer W.C. Handy, Nat Cole prepared carefully. A lot of hopes were riding on this one—

hopes that the all-black musical would come back. (Carmen preceded it; Porgy and Bess followed.)

was that they liked turning on their television sets and see an easy, relaxed show with great music, a charismatic Nat with a happy glitter in his slanted eyes, elegant and charming, offering soft, beguiling music, and famous guest stars.

Later on, he said, "I know what TV is doing. They are freezing the Negro out..."

Without publicity, he kept fighting "on the inside." He was all too aware of the little snubs, little insults—and he realized that when he, who was rich and famous, experienced this every day, his brothers and sisters who had little in the way of material things and power were dealt the same thing in greater amounts and intensity.

Slowly things were beginning to change. For instance, more black people were appearing as guests on television. But Nat wanted to see black people as hosts of their own shows and having prominent parts in good dramas and comedies. He was right about high-prestige sponsors (DuPoint, the Bell Telephone Hour) having more guts than others.

He made sure that he was fighting issues rather than people and demonstrated this by going back to hotels he had sued and staying there. "It's a matter of principle. I'm not mad at the people."

A picture of an enormously fair person emerges. Also an exceedingly well-organized person (a fact that showed even in the impeccable way he was dressed) who did not like when things did not roll along just about perfectly. Next after Maria, his valet/assistant manager Sparky was enormously valuable. Nat did listen to Maria and he was taking her advice in nearly everything except perhaps in matters dealing directly with his music. When it came to music, he knew precisely what he wanted, but concerning the many, many details around his performing, he would welcome intelligent input, especially from her.

In the mid-50s, rock'n'roll was beginning to enter the musical scene, competing with pop tunes.

Nat was intensely aware that trends come and go and that styles in everything, be it fashion or music, are ever changing.

He was keeping up with jazz and bebop to some extent, yet retaining the intimate, gentle feeling of his own music. Rock'n'roll perplexed him; the beat was too hard, too monotonous. He felt it was limited musically.

Then he happened to receive a demonstration record of "Send For Me." He listened to it. He called his daughter Natalie into the room and asked her to listen. She smiled and began to dance. Nat decided to record it with Billy May and his orchestra. "Send for Me" became a million-selling hit.

He went out for dinner with a couple of young songwriters, the Sherman Brothers, who had begun to write for him. Over dinner, Nat discussed rock'n'roll, said he didn't really like it and asked their opinion.

When the brothers, Joe and Noel, drove home, Noel said. "Hey, how about writing something special for Nat? 'Mr. Cole Won't Rock and Roll'!"

The brothers wrote the song and then spent some nail-biting time wondering if Nat would do it. But he liked it and tried it out in Chicago, at the Chez Paree, in the fall of 1959. Again, the Sherman Brothers waited with baited breath. If people in Chicago liked it, Nat would bring it to the Copacabana in New York where he was going next. He did and the song hit, as people were enjoying the lyrics talking about baritones starting to sound more "frantic" than "romantic," and the music having a rock'n'roll flavor.

The Sherman brothers were regarding Nat as a mentor and a friend. They found him unaffected, straightforward and a lot of fun. They used to go to sports events together. Outside of being with his family, going to ball games with a couple of buddies were just about the only times of total relaxation his enormously busy life offered.

Not even those close to him were realizing how the pressures were building around him: Phones were ringing constantly, people kept stopping him in the street, asking for autographs or favors, friends or friends of friends had a multitude of requests. All day, every day, was filled with hundreds of small and big demands. And just about every night he was stepping out on a stage, presenting the picture of the perfectly relaxed, at ease, polite, happy performer—the same image he was unwaveringly presenting to interviewers. He was a man of immense self-control. He was the King.

Chapter Eleven

Wanderlust

(recorded in June 1964)

Nat Cole always wanted to try something new. Other singers had become actors—such as a Bing Crosby, a Frank Sinatra—so why not he? In 1953, he had been a supporting player in *Song for a Banjo* with Dick Haymes in the lead as a farmhand who was befriended by a piano player in jail (Nat), having fought with his band leader. Nat's character helped Dick Haymes's character to clear his name. In another film that year, *Small Town Girl,* he had played himself in one scene, singing "Flaming Heart."

He had starred in the film (rather a

In the film Cat Ballou, starring Lee Marvin, Nat Cole and Stubby Kaye were two cowboy minstrels, complete with banjos, providing a running musical commentary.

featurette) for Universal International, about himself, narrated by Jeff Chandler: *The Nat King Cole Story,* in 1955. It covered his legendary beginning, and his crisis when bleeding ulcers brought him low. He sang five songs in the film, beginning with "Straighten Up and Fly Straight" and "Sweet Lorraine" and ending with "Je Vous Aime."

In 1957, the film *China Gate* with Angie Dickinson and Gene Barry opened—in it Nat played a legionnaire in Vietnam. He also sang the title song.

In *St. Louis Blues* (1958), he played W.C. Handy—with Eartha Kitt as Gog Germain and Pearl Bailey as Aunt Hagar, Ella Fitzgerald as herself, Cab Calloway as Blade and also featuring Mahalia Jackson and Ruby Dee. The *Los Angeles Herald Examiner* said about Nat's performance that it was "laced with dignity and charm."

In *The Night of the Quarter Moon,* shot later that year, he played a nightclub owner and sang one tune. John Drew Barrymore played the lead.

It was a different experience to him. In a recording studio, he was in command; in a film studio, he had to obey; there were constant delays, he was certainly not in command, just had to wait until called.

His music seemed to mean more to audiences—and probably to him—than the acting. *Blue Gardenia* and *Cat Ballou* are a couple of films where especially his singing added life and energy.

Carlos Gastel liked the word "international" and organized a trip to Cuba where Nat performed in Spanish. He did not speak Spanish but had learned to sing phonetically in Spanish and to say a few words. "When you say 'thank you' to a foreigner, it's more gracious to say it in his language, not yours," said ever gracious Nat, who was a big hit at the Tropicana nightclub in Havana, one of the favorite exotic places in the world of many travelers. (This was shortly before the revolution and Castro.) He made a record, *Señor Cole Español*, which became enormously popular throughout Latin America. He was invited to perform at a concert in Brazil in 1960, to which 60,000 enthusiastic fans came, and then made two more records: *A Mis Amigos* in Spanish and Portuguese, and *More Cole Español* which he recorded in Mexico City. Latin stars joined him on *A Mis Amigos*.

His Latin-American fans were so numerous and demonstrative that wherever he went police had to protect him from his admirers.

The year was 1959, Carol was fourteen (and

appreciated her father's indulgence when she mainly wanted to listen to rock'n'roll), and Natalie was nine years old. Since Maria had not become pregnant, in July that year they adopted a beautiful baby boy, born in February (the same month that the Coles had put in their application for adoption). They chose the name Nat Kelly Cole for him, giving him the same initials as his father.

Nat loved his little boy, as he loved Natalie and Carol, but there was little time for him to spend with his family, especially since this was the period when he traveled a lot internationally. Whenever he was at home, he spent all possible time with them (visitors to the house say that he always had one child or another by his hand or in his arms when they came over). "A man should be around the house to help bring up his own children," he said, somewhat wistfully.

In 1960, Nat performed at Victoria Palace Theatre for Queen Elizabeth and Prince Philip. Sweetie and Cookie were old enough to travel to England and to feel pride in their father (although they were too young for the gala reception after the performance).

In Europe, Norman Granz asked Nat to give a helping hand to a young jazz musician by name of Quincy Jones, the leader of a band that had found itself stranded without funds. Quincy joined as the opening band act (about 40 minutes) for Nat King Cole's tour in Sweden, Denmark, France, Italy, Germany, and Switzerland.

In Switzerland the audience seemed restless. "They want you to play more piano," said Quincy. He was right. Nat did some songs as piano solos, and the audience went wild.

A great time was had in Paris, and Nat got along so well with Capitol's man in France that he employed him as road manager for the rest of Europe and as he went on to Asia.

Back in the U.S., Nat was invited to perform at the White House, where he was treated with great respect. This was one of the definite highlights of his career.

He and Harry Belafonte had been thinking and talking of producing films and shows and even formed Cole-Belafonte Enterprises (having flipped a coin to decide which name should come first), but for one reason or another this didn't work out. The two entertainers remained good friends, having enormous respect for each other's talents.

Nat formed his own company, Kell-Cole Productions, which handled all of his ventures from then on. The lawyer Leo Branton, Jr. set it up, bringing Ike Jones in as creative direc-

Sing it, Nat! Talent, like gold, is where you find it. And there was a "glory hold" strike, the pure vein, in Nat King Cole.

When he came on the screen, as in Cat Ballou, *his last film, singing in that satin-husky voice, the magic was there.*

tor. In 1961, they produced a Nat King Cole special, *Wild is Love,* which was aired successfully in Canada the same year. It did not air in the United States until 1964 after one brief segment was cut out: showing Nat putting his arm around Larry Kert, a Canadian performer. The sponsors (again) did not like that a white man and a black man were shown having physical contact for a few seconds!

All these changes were pushing old loyal Carlos Gastel into the background. Although he was continuing as Nat's manager, he and the new people sometimes had conflicting ideas about numerous details.

Nat was beginning to think seriously of Broadway and consequently became involved with the show *I'm With You* with an interracial cast and an original score written by lyricist Dorothy Wayne and composer Ray Rasch. (The two had written the album "Wild Is Love.") Since Kell-Cole productions were searching for a musical vehicle for Nat, Dotty wrote seventeen songs with Ray; these would be connected by dialogue. The theme of the show was man's search for love.

The lovely and radiant singer Barbara McNair played the female lead, and the premiere was held on October 30, 1960, in San Francisco. The reviews were lukewarm. Nat and Barbara tried to work on the dialogue connecting the songs since they felt that there lay the problem—and possibly also in the interracial cast.

Nat who had dreamt of opening on Broadway was feeling down and showing it, which was unusual for him. Barbara suggested that they take one day off, just to relax, but instead she was finding out how impossible that was for someone as famous as Nat. They set out for Sausalito but Nat was accosted by enthusiastic admirers everywhere. They went to a restaurant and weren't allowed to pay the bill. Barbara suggested that Nat should disguise himself by wearing old clothes, but he resisted, feeling people would say, "Look, there's Nat Cole looking like a bum."

Maria and the children came to try to cheer him up, and that helped. With renewed energy on Nat's part, lots of changes were made, and the show went on the road. Nearly everybody seemed to be falling apart. Dotty Wayne herself left the show in exasperation, but Nat just kept trying to make it better, never showing bad tempers. He and Barbara McNair stuck it out, and the two of them were getting along exceptionally well. She was amazed at his totally perfect pitch; perhaps you have to be a singer yourself to really appreciate that a man could take any note out of the air and deliver it absolutely right and clear.

Barbara knew the show wasn't good, but her admiration for the man who gave it everything he had in him made her stay on until it closed on November 26, 1960. In early December, he announced that the show would be completely redone under the title *Wandering Man*. Rehearsals would begin by January 10, 1961, and he was planning to open on Broadway in late February.

The theme remained unchanged but new songs had been added. Nat was putting his own money on the line because the earlier sponsors and producers had withdrawn one by one. He had employed a new director, a new choreographer, and forty singers and dancers. However, the first week in January he was forced to announce that this Broadway dream of his would not become reality. But if not Broadway, why not the Greek Theater in Los Angeles? thought he, removed nearly all of the narrative, added more singing and dancing, and presented it as *Sights and Sounds: The Merry World of Nat King Cole*. In that show, Natalie Cole performed as a professional for the first time. She had already impressed her father by her understanding of singing and music and her personal way of interpreting a

Gentle and soft-spoken, yes, but he was not as detached and quiet as he frequently was described. He was gentle but there were deep passions in this man. Deep angers at injustice, too.

song. (Her absolute favorites were Ella Fitzgerald and Nancy Wilson with Carmen McRae and Sarah Vaughan as close seconds.)

In the show she played a young version of herself, singing the song "It's a Bore," for which she received $600; Barbara McNair then played her as grown-up.

The show received excellent reviews.

And life handed the Coles a little surprise— or rather two: Maria had become pregnant (fifteen months after adopting Kelly). On September 26, 1961, at St. John's Hospital in Santa Monica, Maria gave birth to identical twin girls, whom they named Timolin (the name was suggested by songwriter Johnny Burke) and Casey (after Casey Stengel).

With three small children and two of school age, Maria was more and more electing to stay home when Nat went on the road. He was doing his best to give all he could to his family whenever his time would allow, and the children, especially the two older girls, cherished the good times with their father. Each of them had a special relationship with him.

Maria had bought Nat a birthday present one year, an XKE Jaguar sports car which he drove so fast that nobody except Natalie would get into it with him, both of them singing and laughing.

In 1961 Carol was to be presented by a national black women's sorority at a debutantes' ball at the Beverly Hilton Hotel. The very same evening President John F. Kennedy was honored at a dinner at Hollywood Palladium, and Nat had been invited to perform. He went to the dinner, made his appearance on the dais with the president, then explained to Kennedy that he had to leave to present his daughter at the ball at the Hilton and left. Whereupon Kennedy made a surprise appearance at the ball later in the evening ("Nat sang at our dinner tonight, so I thought I'd reciprocate"), greeting all the debutantes but paying special attention to Carol.

In 1962, Nat received a tune called "Ramblin' Rose" from the Sherman brothers. He liked the hint of country in it—some people at the recording studio did not agree at all and recommended that he not include it in his new recording. But when it came to his songs and his music, nobody could tell Nat anything. He recorded it, and it sold a million records very fast, becoming his first enormous hit after several years of "medium hits."

A funny story is told about how he was being interviewed on radio somewhere in the South, and the interviewer praised "Ramblin'

Rose" as an authentic Southern song with authentic Southern feelings. Nat let him go on and on. Then he said quietly, "Actually, it was written by two Jewish boys from Brooklyn." He and the Sherman brothers had a good laugh about that later. (Joe Sherman who wrote the music for it in eighteen minutes received royalties for the next thirty years).

1962 marked the twenty-fifth anniversary of Nat's trio, and Capitol Records and the Los Angeles chapter of the Urban League sponsored a tribute to him at the Ambassador Hotel. Hollywood's luminaries came: Doris Day, Art Linkletter, Jerry Lewis, Groucho Marx, Mickey Rooney, Robert Stack, Connie Stevens, Gene Barry, Rosemary Clooney and more. Sammy Cahn wrote special songs for the event, Mahalia Jackson performed, Earl "Fatha" Hines spoke glowingly, and Dick Gregory and Dick Shawn ribbed Nat unmercifully. Steve Allen was master of ceremonies and, since Marilyn Monroe had died only hours earlier, a shock to the Hollywood community, Allen remarked that it was a great satisfaction to honor a man while he could be there to receive their affection.

Nat decided to take *Sights and Sounds: The Merry World of Nat King Cole* out on the road where it continued to reap success. The show played in more than one hundred cities across the country, including cities in Kentucky, Maryland, and Tennessee, his first performances in the South since his 1956 tour. The fact that his integrated Merry Young Souls were allowed to perform on the stages of the South was a hopeful sign to him.

Sometimes this was not as easily accomplished as it might sound. There was the time his producer, Ike Jones, came to Nat and told him that the owner of one of the West Coast's top hotels wanted them to bring the integrated musical into his fancy inn for three weeks and would pay a substantial bonus provided that Nat and Jones would recast the show and make it an all-black divertissement. Jones confidently expected Cole to turn the offer down instantly. Instead, Nat seemed to weigh the proposal for a couple of minutes. Then he said, "You tell Mr. Charlie. . .just tell him we'll be glad to make this an all-colored show. Provided he agrees to staff his whole hotel with Negroes while we're there."

All of 1963 he traveled with *Sights and Sounds,* while his "Those Crazy Lazy Hazy Days of Summer," a simple tune, became a million-selling record.

Chapter Twelve

Brush Those Tears From Your Eyes

(recorded in May 1964)

A major change in the 1960s was that Nat fired his manager Carlos Gastel some time in 1964. "The only bad thing Nat Cole ever did," in Sparky's opinion. Maria had taken over more of his business along with the lawyer Leo Branton and producer Ike Jones, and they felt that Carlos had outgrown his usefulness. An added reason was that Carlos, always a heavy drinker, was drinking even more than before.

Nat had appeared at the White House during the Eisenhower years, then again for President Kennedy; the two men had a ge-

---

He was only forty-five when he died, but most people insisted, when they read the obituaries, that he had to be older because it seemed as if that incredible voice had been around forever...

nuine liking for each other. In January 1964, Cole visited with President Johnson, pledging him his support as he had been supporting President Kennedy in his own way. "As a professional entertainer, not as a professional Negro," he is said to have expressed it. "The first thing I'm fighting for is individualism," he said another time, wanting blacks to fight by being recognized for talents, intelligence and achievement.

He went to England with his family, except for the twins who were too young to go. The tour over there was highly successful—the teenagers responded to all the recent hits he sang, the romantics loved "To the End of the Earth" and "Hi Lili, Hi Lo." Those who revered him mainly as a musician hooted when he sat down and played the piano, never having lost one iota of his masterly touch. He ended every concert with "Let There Be Love," pouring all his hopes for the world into it.

One gets a picture of a man who sang of love but who felt lonely. Many blacks of the time did not understand why he did not take a more active part in civil rights issues, why he showed no militancy and anger. His marriage of seventeen years was feeling the strain of him being gone so much of the time. One biographer of Nat Cole, James Haskins, says, "All who talk about the trouble between Nat and Maria mention Las Vegas."

Why Las Vegas? The gambling? Possibly. It is said that he and Sammy Davis Jr. went gambling and sometimes dropping a few thousand dollars on the tables. Nat's attitude about money was still somewhat careless—he had his voice, he had his music, he could always make a living.

Women? There must have been more temptations in a week than most men encounter in a lifetime. Nat was representing a heartfelt sensuality, and in Las Vegas everything tends to take on a frenzied quality. He was always surrounded by adoring people in Las Vegas. Not the least white women showed their admiration openly, at times aggressively. Maria had stopped accompanying him there, hating the place and all it stood for.

In 1964 he arrived in New York City for his annual Copacabana engagement. Maria, not knowing he didn't feel well, did not come along. He had told no one on his staff how poorly he felt. Carol, who had graduated from college and was pursuing a stage career, came to see him in New York, but he told her nothing. He was staying in the apartment near Lincoln Center that he and Maria had bought (again through an intermediary of white skin

The material legends are made of. . . When Nat King Cole toured Europe in 1960, he was asked to lend a helping hand to a young jazz musician whose band was stranded without funds.

Nat did, and a certain Quincy Jones (here with Ray Charles)
became Nat's forty minute opening band act for the tour to
Sweden, Denmark, France, Italy, Germany, Switzerland.

color). The Sherman brothers, both living nearby, used to go over to watch sports games with Nat. "I've been having a terrible backache for a while," he told them once. During the rest of his engagement he never mentioned his back pain again but spoke of his daughter Natalie and her desire to get into show business.

He went on to Las Vegas, and now the people working for him started to worry, since he began to go directly to his room after each show. Normally he liked to unwind by going somewhere and hanging out with friends.

His back was hurting so much that he had trouble walking. A doctor was called to his hotel, and an electrocardiogram showed that there was nothing wrong with his heart.

From Las Vegas he went to Harrah's in Lake Tahoe. He was losing weight rapidly; he was chronically tired but blamed it on his work schedule which remained intense: During the summer and early fall of 1964, he appeared with *Sights and Sounds* in Lake Tahoe every night, and every day he flew to Los Angeles where he was filming *Cat Ballou*, starring Lee Marvin. He and Stubby Kaye, as two minstrels dressed as cowboys, provided a running musical commentary on what was happening on the screen and sang "The Ballad of Cat

Ballou," plucking banjos. This meant that Nat mainly slept on the plane taking him back and forth between Lake Tahoe and Los Angeles.

When the film was finished, Nat went on to his next engagement in San Francisco. He stayed at the Fairmont Hotel, felt sicker and sicker, the hotel physician examined him, and ordered an X-ray which revealed a tumor on his left lung. Nat's first reaction was to keep working and not to tell Maria who was in Europe.

He finished out his engagement although he had to be helped up the stairs of the theater. Then he went back to Los Angeles. He called Maria in London and mentioned casually that he was checking into St. John's Hospital in Santa Monica but he did not tell her why. She flew back immediately and took charge.

Determinedly, Maria made optimistic statements to the press and public that Nat Cole was having cobalt treatments for lung cancer, and the outlook was good. In reality, it was not. He had entered the hospital in December and was too weak to go home for Christmas. His children were allowed to come to him instead, finding him in an unusually bad mood. He was in terrible pain, he was depressed. Only Carol and Natalie were old enough to understand.

Natalie Cole is carrying the musical torch of Nat King Cole into the 1990s. Here she is on stage at Las Vegas Tropicana

*Hotel as she and Lou Rawls enjoy a Bill Cosby monologue, all
to benefit the United Negro College fund.*

Mail was pouring in from all over the world. Fellow entertainers sent messages of hope, such as John Wayne who had battled lung cancer and won.

Nat went home for two days over the New Year's, attended by nurses around the clock. The pain forced him back to the hospital. The outpouring of love of which the deluge of mail bore witness made him brighten momentarily.

But the tumors were spreading. On January 25, 1965, his left lung was removed. Again, Maria lied to the newspapers, sounding optimistic.

Nat's father in Chicago was also seriously ill, and the news of his son's grave illness was kept from him. Nat called him from the hospital, pretending to be calling from home and managing to sound cheerful. On February 1st, the Reverend Coles died. Nat said little when told, but it seemed he took an immediate turn for the worse.

Frank Sinatra was a frequent visitor to the hospital, but most other visitors had to be cut out because Nat didn't have the strength to see them. Maria, ever at his bedside and ever trying to cheer him up, spoke of buying a cottage by the beach in Santa Monica where he could recuperate. This made him smile and say that he was going to start practice playing the organ.

On February 14, Valentine's Day, he seemed better, the weather was gorgeous, and Maria took him for a ride to the Santa Monica shore, along went her sister Charlotte and a nurse. They brought him back in a good mood, and he went to sleep. At dawn he died.

He was a month and two days away from his forty-sixth birthday.

The date was February 15. More than a million of Nat's records were ordered from Capitol between his death and his funeral on February 18.

There was room for only four hundred persons inside St. James' but another three thousand were standing outside, many crying openly.

Jack Benny delivered the eulogy about the man "who gave so much and still had so much more to give. Sometimes death isn't as tragic as not knowing how to live. This nice man knew how to live and knew how to make others glad they were living." George Jessel spoke about the fact that Nat had been the first black man to become a member of the Friar's Club, the entertainers' organization. "Sweet dreams, good man..."

His friends came to pay their last respect: Frank Sinatra, who was a pall bearer, Cab

Calloway, Duke Ellington, Jack Benny, Henry Miller, Stan Kenton, Ricardo Montalban, George Burns, Nelson Riddle, Peter Lawford, Edward G. Robinson, Johnny Mathis, Jimmy Durante, Governor Edmund Brown of California, Senator Robert F. Kennedy of New York, Count Basie. . . Sammy Davis, Jr. canceled his performance in "Golden Boy" on Broadway to fly to the funeral. Jerry Lewis, Gene Barry, Danny Thomas, Vic Damone, Frankie Laine, Eddie "Rochester" Anderson, Bobby Darin, Jose Ferrer, Rosemary Clooney, Dorothy Dandridge (the godmother of the twins). . .The children surrounded their mother: Cookie who was about twenty-one, Natalie, fifteen and still a student in a private school, Kelly, a sensitive and brave six, and the three-and-a-half year-old twin girls, Timolin and Casey. Sparky, who had become Nancy Wilson's road manager, since he wasn't needed during Nat's illness, flew in from Florida. Oscar Moore, Joe Comfort, Irving Ashby, Charlie Harris, John Collins—most of Nat's old colleagues came. Those who couldn't make it to the West Coast went to St. Thomas Episcopal Church on Fifth Avenue, where just about everyone in the East Coast music business gathered at the same time the service was taking place on the West Coast.

The world, shocked at the news, mourned the death of Nat King Cole.

An editorial in the *Birmingham News* in Alabama described him as an entertainer of "good taste and style."

The common sentiment was (and is): Nat King Cole is gone; King Cole will live as long as those grooves hold a needle and those tapes retain a sound.

Joseph Campbell has said, "Follow your bliss." Nat King Cole did indeed; he lived his potentiality.

Or as he said in the closing line of his last show (a favorite expression of his in private, too): "Enjoy yourself. Because when you're dead—when you're dead life just ain't worth living."

I Hear Music

(recorded in June 1955)

The music goes on . . .

In 1990, during the Grammy Awards ceremony, Maria Cole accepted the Lifetime Achievement Award on behalf of her husband; the audience showing that he had not been forgotten during the twenty-five years he had been gone.

Maria Cole had remained active during this time. She had taken care of Nat King Cole's complicated estate, fulfilled some of his dreams such as producing James Baldwin's play *Amen Corner,* and forming the Nat King Cole Cancer Foundation. For a while she

---

Natalie Cole did not just inherit musicality from her father—she inherited considerable strength as well. She has moved through "a sea of trouble" and come out a winner.

resumed her singing career, helped by among others Duke Ellington and Ed Sullivan. But she quit, feeling that as the widow of the King she did not want to appear in anything but the top clubs. She co-hosted a radio show for a while, and she wrote *Nat King Cole: An Intimate Biography* which was published in 1971. She donated photographs and correspondence of her husband to the Doheny Library at the University of Southern California. In 1971 she also remarried. Her husband was a screenwriter, and the marriage lasted about five years.

And the children. . . all of whom graduated from college. . .

Cookie had started as an actress, first on stage; she was accepted into a contract-player program at Columbia Studios but then chose a domestic life style with husband and two children.

Kelly Cole was just six when his father died. Edward G. Robinson became sort of a surrogate father to him along with Bing Crosby and other family friends. He grew into a handsome man with a strong interest in production and considerable writing ability. The twin girls, Timolin and Casey, have sought anonymity to a great extent but seem to be leading successful lives.

Natalie has, of course, continued in the best Cole tradition, doing her father's memory proud, as if destined for this life. By age five she had been on Art Linkletter's television show "Kids Say the Darndest Things" twice. At eleven she made her first stage appearance at the Greek Theater in Los Angeles. In high school she planned to become a doctor for a while, but her father's death might have propelled her toward a career in show business. She made her first professional appearance as a singer in 1971. In 1973 she played the Copacabana for the first time. She has had problems with polyps on her throat, with drugs, with divorce—but she has licked it all. She is a survivor, and she is presently enjoying greater success than ever with her "Unforgettable" recording of twenty-four of her father's songs, capped by an irresistible, electronically arranged duet with his voice on the title song. "These songs are a gift from my father," she has said in interviews. Or to quote her special thanks in the liner notes: "This project has touched all of us deeply, and it has left a smile on my face that will not go away anytime soon. I hope you feel the same. So sit back and enjoy, and, by the way...thanks Dad..."

CHRONOLOGY

1919 Born in Montgomery, Alabama, on March 17, as Nathaniel Adams Coles

1923 The Coles family moves to Chicago

1927 His brother Ike is born

1929 Nat enters a musical contest at the Regal Theater and wins first prize, a turkey; his oldest sister, Eddie Mae, dies of pneumonia

1931 His brother Lionel (Freddy) is born

1935 Nat organizes two musical groups: a big band, Nat Coles and His Rogues of Rhythm, and a quintet, Nat Coles and His Royal Dukes

1936 Nat and his brother Eddie play the Panama Club in Chicago; make recordings with Decca's Sepia Series; Nat goes on tour with "Shuffle Along" and marries Nadine Robinson

1937 Nat and Nadine try to make a go of it in Los Angeles

1938 Nat's first trio plays professionally at the Sewanee Inn, Los Angeles. Nat writes "Straighten Up and Fly Right"

1940 Nat records with Lionel Hampton. Cole's Swingsters record four songs

1941 The Nat King Cole trio record for Decca, and Nat is singing

1943 Carlos Gastel becomes the trio's manager and gets them a seven year recording contract with Capitol

1944 Nat plays jazz at the Philharmonic Auditorium under the name Shorty Nadine

1946 The song "Gee Baby, Ain't I Good to You" rises to ninth place on the charts; Nat meets Maria Ellington; Nat begins doing the radio show, "The Wildroot Cream Oil Show" (lasting until early 1949)

1948 Nat's divorce from Nadine becomes final; Nat and Maria marry; "Nature Boy" becomes the number-one hit in the U.S.; Maria's sister Carol dies; Maria and Nat adopt her daughter also named Carol, called Cookie

1950	Maria gives birth to Natalie Maria, called Sweetie
1951	The Internal Revenue go after Nat for $146,000 in back taxes and order the $85,000 Cole home seized
1953	Nat is a supporting player in a couple of films; undergoes surgery for bleeding stomach ulcers
1954	Nat signs a three year contract at the Sands in Las Vegas; performs in top clubs in New York, Los Angeles and Chicago. Gives concerts in France and England
1955	Maria opens in a night club act; Nat stars in a featurette about himself, *The Nat King Cole Story*
1956	Nat is the victim of a vicious racist attack, luckily largely averted, during a concert in Birmingham, Alabama; stars in his own 15-minute television show
1957	Nat's television show is expanded to half an hour; Nat plays in "China Gate" and sings the title song of the movie; Nat tours Australia
1958	Nat plays in "St. Louis Blues" and "The Night of the Quarter Moon"
1959	Nat performs in Cuba; Nat and Maria adopt Nat Kelly Cole
1960	Nat performs in Brazil and in England, for the Queen. Tours Europe with Quincy Jones as his opening act; the stage show "I'm With You" opens in San Francisco
1961	A Nat King Cole special is aired in Canada; the stage show "Sights and Sounds: The Merry World of Nat King Cole" opens; Natalie Cole performs as a professional for the first time; Maria gives birth to the twin girls Timolin and Casey
1962	A star-studded tribute to Nat on the twenty-fifth anniversary of his trio
1963	Nat is touring with "Sights and Sounds"
1964	Nat tours England, a huge success; films "Cat Ballou;" appears in "Sights and Sounds" in Lake Tahoe: enters St. John's Hospital in Santa Monica with lung cancer
1965	Nat King Cole dies on February 15
1990	Nat King Cole receives the Life Achievement Award at the Grammy Awards

SELECTED DISCOGRAPHY

Nat King Cole recorded many songs every year from 1936 on. This is a partial list of his albums (all on Capitol).

After Midnight—1956
Love Is The Thing—1957
St. Louis Blues—1958
Cole Espanol—1958
Welcome to the Club—1958 (reissued in 1962 as *The Swinging Side of Nat Cole*)
To Whom It May Concern—1958
Everytime I Feel the Spirit—1958
A Mis Amigos—1959
Nat King Cole at the Sands (recorded 1960, issued in 1966)
Wild Is Love—1960
The Magic of Christmas—1960
The Touch of Your Lips—1961
The Nat King Cole Story—1961
The Very Thought of You—1961
Nat Cole Sings, George Shearing Plays—1961
Let's Face the Music—1962
Where Did Everyone Go?—1962
Dear Lonely Hearts—1962
Tell Me All About Yourself—1963
Those Lazy-Hazy-Crazy Days of Summer—1963
My Fair Lady—1964
I Don't Want to Be Hurt Anymore—1964
L-O-V-E—1965
The Unreleased Nat King Cole—1987
The Piano Style of Nat King Cole—1990

INDEX

189

190

PICTURE CREDITS

Original pen/ink drawings by Christopher de Gasperi.
Eddie Brandt's Saturday Matinee: 16, 21, 24, 48, 64,
68, 74, 80, 87, 92, 96, 100, 114, 132, 137, 138, 144, 150,
156, 160, 110, Warner Brothers: Photo by Ron Wolfson,
170; Photograph by Ray Locke: 28-29; Universal-
International; 126; Players International: 35, 39, 59.